CO
OR
GOD?

A TESTIMONY
ILLUSTRATING
THERE IS A
LIVING GOD

AARON GARCIA

Cover Designer:

Laura Hidalgo, www.BookfabulousDesigns.com

Editing:

Tiffany Tillman, www.RedheadBookServices.com

e-Book & Print Layout :

Deena Schoenfeldt, www.e-bookbuilders.com

Write us!
 P.O. Box 364
Diamond, MO 64840

Contents

Dedication

This book is dedicated to my beautiful wife, Emily, who is my rock and my soulmate. Words can't describe the love that I have for you. May this be the first journey of the rest of our lives. Always and forever Emily, to the moon and back.

Introduction

Have you ever looked at your life and thought it was a coincidence? No, seriously. Stop what you're doing right now and weigh out all of your past experiences, memories, and chapters of your life and ponder if you were placed on this earth for a reason. Or do things magically happen because of luck? Did you get the image? We all wonder about the reason for life. Some skeptics believe we are living one big dream, while others believe it's simply fate. What's your perspective? Do you believe we merely exist out of pure luck? Do you believe we just go through the motions and that's it? It's finished? Over? Kaput? End of story?

Your life isn't made of concurrent events or circumstances that have no apparent connection. No, your life was meant to be spectacular, with purpose and a plan! Even before you were born, you were named, and before you were named, you were created. But what is creation and why were we created? In this book you will find the answers to your questions and proof of why you exist through my living, transformed testimony. Sure, you have heard a lot of testimonies and stories of what God has done in other people's lives, but this one will provide you with truth about a living God who exists and desires to know His children.

You are about to embark on a story so life-changing, so miraculous, so Heaven-sent that by the time you finish there will be no question in your mind about God's existence. You have bought your ticket to a front row seat for a glimpse into a realm so unknown, most Christians dare not go. Actually, most Christians have never seen this side of the spiritual world. I'm talking about a place which is very dark—so dark you can't even see the silhouette of your hand in front of your face. It is a place so evil it would send terror and fear even into the eyes of the unsaved. I must warn you that this testimony will, at times, make you uncomfortable, but I want to open your eyes to a world which most people have never seen, let alone visited. We are at war for our souls in the spiritual realm, and I've seen it. But alas, even the least bit of light pushes the darkness away.

I have prayed diligently over this book and it's no coincidence it's in your possession now. Everything happens for a reason, and that reason is because God orchestrated it. People, situations, memories, difficulties, trials, and tribulations all enter your life because He wants to establish faith and hope in your life. He is maturing you one situation at a time. Whatever is meant to be bad, God uses for good. Whether you're a believer or non-believer, Atheist or Christian, saved or unsaved, searching or not, this book is for everyone. This testimony is completely real. Everything you will read happened. I had to change the names in this story to protect the innocent, but I assure you my life is not a coincidence; it is the opposite. My life was meant for a purpose, just like your life was meant for a purpose—a meaningful, planned, God-given purpose. I like to call it your destiny. By the time you finish this book, you will understand your life is by no means a big series of coincidences.

1

Where It All Began

As a child, I grew up in a normal household. It was just my mother, father, and my brother, who was five years younger than me, all in a single-family home. We grew up in the Methodist Church. The church we attended was a rustic church, which was very old in appearance, and the entire congregation consisted of family members. It was like one big, happy, family reunion every Sunday during service. Growing up, I followed the routine church family schedule. We went to church every Sunday because Mother always wanted us to. As a younger child, my seat was toward the front of the building, but as the years progressed I found myself toward the back of the pews, socializing with my peers. We would sit back there doodling random pictures and challenging each other to tic-tac-toe games while bypassing worship and the spoken Word. Being a part of the church, camp attendance was encouraged. I went to church camp because my family wanted what was best for me. But sometimes the best still isn't good enough.

Church camp is supposed to be a pleasant place where you can build relationships and grow with God. Unfortunately, I didn't get that pleasant experience, but an unpleasant surprise. My cottage consisted of ten young men. These guys never attended my church. Most of the guys, it appeared, already had formed their clique, and they weren't about to make me a part of it. It was not because of my choice, but because of their choices. It's unfortunate, but these guys who were in my cottage to help me grow in Christ were the same ones who bullied me for the next week. They constantly picked at and prodded me in different group settings and at night would physically beat me. This was not like the typical "soap party" beating you see in military movies where they throw a blanket over you and beat you with soap attached to rope. No, they beat me every night with their closed fists as I cried myself to sleep. Every night. I lost track of the days bypassing me. It was one big nightmare with no ending. I would wake up with bruises and swelling that were obvious, but no one ever said anything. It was terrible. I was numb at times from the physical beatings. These villains found satisfaction in my suffering. They found pride in my punishment. My pain was their release. They continuously tortured me throughout the week and I said nothing—not to a counselor, not to my other peers, and especially not to my parents. I was stuck in a Christian prison where I had come to get deliverance in the first place. I would lie there at night, anticipating when my next punishment would be. It didn't come at scheduled times during the night; it always came at times I least expected it. So I would lie there, trembling in my bed, while the others laughed at my fear. I stared at the wooden beams of the cabin while I fearfully waited for my next blow.

How could this be happening to me? Does God see my suffering? Does He even care? I just want to go home. I want this nightmare to be over. Please, God, take away all that has happened to me and get me back to safety.

Finally, the end of the week came and I was delivered from my prison only because church camp was over. I wasn't saved from evil or lent a hand of sympathy.

My parents were the ones who picked me up at the front gate, but I wasn't about to speak about what I had experienced. They simply asked, "So, how was camp?"

If they had only known the torture and pain I had endured back at that godforsaken place they would have pulled the vehicle around and rampaged right through the front gates. But I just sat there and said, "Everything went great, I had a good time!" Oh, I couldn't have lied any better. That was the last time I ever attended church camp.

Have you ever come to a situation or crisis in your life in which you didn't feel the grace of God? That was me that week at church camp. I was a boy who wanted to grow closer to God but felt betrayed by the very place which was supposed to bring him peace.

◆
◆ ◆
◆

I'll never forget the first day I saw her. Her appearance filled the room. Her markings were so apparent that I couldn't deny she was meant for beauty. She wore a cherry red exterior and her finish was blinding, as though she was created brand new. Her shoes matched the outfit. I mean, what woman doesn't love matching shoes? I saw her personality in her tangible presence. The mold was broken when they made her and she was undeniably attractive.

"She" was a 1990 Toyota Tercel, and best of all, she was all mine.

I was fifteen years old when my parents had decided to purchase my first car. Let me tell you, if you're as insane as to purchase your child's first car like my parents did, you may want to reevaluate your mental status. I had never owned, let alone operated, a pile of metal that traveled at highway speeds ever in my entire life. Who in their right mind would allow this teenage boy who had never worked a day in his life, the privilege of driving a vehicle? Okay, I was a working teenage boy, but I never put a dime of my own money into this vehicle.

I was sixteen years old when I landed my first job. Although I thought I could be anything I set my mind to, I decided to lay down my pride and become a sandwich artist instead. Just think of the name "sandwich artist." I was an up-and-coming artist just like Picasso once was, except from a culinary arts perspective. I put my first application in, and eureka! I was offered the job one week later. It was a great first job and I was on cloud nine.

The owner was very kind and accepting. Her wavy blond hair was like that from a bad 80s hair band, but oddly, it fit her. She always wore a smile when she walked through the store, and she was willing to help any of her employees without any hesitation. She kind of resembled my mother in the caring nature she had. Although I knew better than to ever ask a woman her age, I assumed she was in the same age bracket as my mother based on her physical features.

I worked very close beside two college girls who were already employed there. I considered myself a charmer with them because I could say anything to these two women and their hearts would melt. I realized later that they thought I was a cute kid and found me adorable, which, for us men, really shoots down one's self-esteem. But I took it for what it was worth. I got the attention I craved and they got some sort of sick entertainment out of me.

We three were like family. We worked hard together. Like a three man Olympic rowing team, we encouraged each other with each stroke as we coasted down the river. As a team, we helped establish a name and a reputation for the store—the reputation of gratitude with an abundance of customer service. We were always busy, but that was okay. I considered it job security. The store was located near a busy main street so the flow of people never stopped. It was like the city opened the flood gates and the people came pouring in. I established great relationships with the usual customers whom I served weekly. I loved people. I loved hard work. It was developing me into a young man with ambition. I'm not trying to toot my own horn here, but I could make a wicked sandwich!

That job lasted about one year. Can you imagine me, on my first foray into the workforce, lasting one year at my first job? I did it. I was well on my way to success, or so I thought. I ended up quitting that job because the store relocated to a more distant location. But what I had established at this job, I carried with me throughout my life. Then, all of a sudden, that door to my future closed and I found myself, once again, jobless.

Teenagers think they know everything. We believe we have it all together and there is nothing you can't tell us that we don't already know. Does this sound familiar? That's because all of us, at one point in time, in our child-like ways, thought like this, and unfortunately some of us still do today. But seriously, teenagers are hard to manage, even when they aren't released into the streets with an oversized vehicle which could cause harm.

Let me back up a little. I didn't even introduce myself. My fault. My name is Aaron, and I'm what you call inquisitive. I have lived most of my life in the Midwest, in a city called Joplin, Missouri. It's the place I call home, for now. I mean you never know where God may take you next. I am currently thirty-two years old and feel young at heart. I believe my age recedes backwards as the birthdays continue. So really, if you want to get technical, I'm a young, sophisticated twenty-one-year-old. I'm random, funny, and surprisingly outgoing (did you catch that joke?). Okay, I'm *severely* outgoing. I don't shut up. I talk all the time and find myself actively trying to shut myself up on occasion. I love people. I love interacting and building new relationships with new people.

Did I mention I'm inquisitive? I love collecting things. I would not call myself a hoarder per se, because I have so much OCD I can go through a bottle of Windex in less than twenty-four hours. I mean that I love retaining information. Everything interests me—books, objects, photographs, memorabilia, and traveling. I collect and retain things because I love information and you never know when those items will be useful. The world is an interesting place because it has infinite variety and complexity. Have you ever noticed the vast amount of information your brain can obtain? Did you know your mind can think up fourteen hundred words per minute? I'm getting nauseated just examining all those words right now, but it is who I am.

I am what you call inclusive. I never want to keep people outside of the circle. Do you remember, as a child, that one time you were picked for kickball, and there was that one kid who was always picked last or not picked at all? I am not this guy. I'm like, "Bro, get over here so I can include you in everything!" I include people so much that sometimes they get uncomfortable being *too* included.

I'm positive. I find the goodness in everything. If you lost your dog, that's okay, you'll get another one. If you didn't get that job, that's okay, it wasn't meant for you. Some people probably find it annoying how positive I am, but once again, it is who I am.

I could go on and on about my characteristics as an individual, but I left out the best part. I saved the best for last. The most important part of who I am is that I am a child of God—the everlasting, all-knowing, all-powerful, infinitely gracious God—who came into my life and saved me from darkness, who adopted me as an abandoned orphan-child saved by grace, and gave me a new name with a new identity.

God is a God of wonder. He is continuously giving. Even when we go through the toughest days, we find strength in Him. I could go on forever about my God, but I will let this story speak for itself.

At sixteen, teenagers start developing relationships with people in high school that become more concrete and fulfilling. Teenagers start forming cliques, and winning popularity contests becomes a mandatory goal. We no longer enjoy each other's company, but instead start to become selfish and focused on our own insecurities. That was me. I was looking for a place to belong, a perfect fit, like a cord plugged in to an outlet. I had just been given my car and used my independence to help search for that place. Oh, how blinded I was by the culture which surrounded me. I didn't know it yet, but that same car I was infatuated with would be the object that cursed me into darkness.

At my high school, reputations became very important. Teenagers started to equate possessions with success. If your family came from money, you were rich. If you owned a flashy car, you were considered popular. Whatever you represented, whether money or image, that's who you were, and your identity is identified by others' perception. I drove a 1990 Toyota Tercel, which was about six years old at the time. The newness of the vehicle meant I represented independence and popularity, which was what every adolescent wanted. People began to notice me. Many of my peers began to approach me to get to know me better. It was great. I was being accepted. What I *didn't* realize was that people didn't like me for me, they wanted what I had. They wanted what I represented. I owned a car, so that meant I represented freedom.

Have you ever wanted something so badly you would do anything to get it? We have so much motivation when it comes to things we want, but we are not willing to push for things that are important in life. We want money, so we scheme our way into becoming financially comfortable. We want to be successful, so we strategize about what investments to make and what personal gain we can obtain if we get to the top. We want to be accepted, so we become something we aren't. Whatever the case may be, we do things we don't feel good about doing, but we do them anyway. What about you? What things do you find yourself doing that you know aren't taking you in the right direction?

The reality is that I was living an artificial life and it drew in bad company. The months went on and I had accumulated a large number of friends. I can't even remember how it happened. It was like I became a well-known speaker and gained an entourage overnight. While all this was going on, I was blinded by who else was stepping foot into my life. As I built new relationships, I met a man who would change my life forever and redirect my steps in the wrong direction—a direction you can't find on any compass or map. This is where it all began.

His name was Jake, and he was mysteriously inviting. His appearance was just like that of any other student, but his words were like finely-tuned instruments. He could sell a ketchup popsicle to any boy with white gloves. He sold me anyway. He sold me with his words of wisdom, and we became best friends.

Jake represented popularity and acceptance, which was what I had been looking for this whole time. Although I was surrounded by many friends, I wanted what Jake had, and that was an image. Jake was independent. He was such an individual that you swore he came from a different continent, like a deserted island. No one else had the characteristics Jake had, because he was bold. I would call him a rebel. Jake came from a broken home—his father no longer lived with his mother, himself, and his siblings. He lived in a poor neighborhood, but he wasn't about to let the status quo affect him. He was bold and brave. Jake didn't care what people thought about him because he was the one calling the shots. I admired him. I admired what he stood for and that he didn't fabricate who he was to others.

Jake and I spent a lot of time together. He introduced me to the hundreds of friends surrounding him. He was like an idol, but without the tenor voice and millions of viewers watching him through the television screen. Women wanted him and men wanted to be what he represented.

Jake and I spoke throughout the week in the hallways and come the weekend, it was on. It was as if someone had turned on the bat-signal, giving us the sign to be released into the streets. It was adventurous. You would swear we resembled Bo and Luke Duke driving the General Lee on the *Dukes of Hazzard*. We would go from house to house and hang with the popular crowds, partying, drinking, and living lavishly. I always tried to keep a sober mind while people were falling, forgetting, and secretly stepping away together into vacant rooms all around me. I was well on my way to being accepted by my fellow peers and creating a name for myself, or so I thought.

The phone rang and I looked at the screen. It was Jake. I was sitting on the edge of the bed, anticipating the call, when I answered the phone in suspense.

"It's time," Jake said. "You ready?"

I hesitated at first, then I replied, "Be there in a minute." Tonight was the night Jake would introduce me to some new friends, some *older* friends. No one else at our school knew these friends because they had supposedly graduated already. I wasn't sure whether or not I believed that yet. Anxiety filled my mind, but I hung up the phone and picked up my car keys as I walked to the front door. I got into my car and closed the door behind me. As I sat there, I breathed deeply and I put the key into the ignition. For some reason, tonight's hangout seemed different. My intuition about the place gave me anxiety and I hadn't even seen it yet. I picked up Jake as usual. Surprisingly, I was the only one with transportation, so I always drove.

Jake told me we were going to a place I had never been before and I was to keep everything I saw tonight to myself. This was a side of Jake I hadn't seen before. He had a detached demeanor about himself, and I was suspicious about the whole trip.

We had pulled up to a street corner. The neighborhood was very quiet, as though no one even lived in the area. The air was foggy and it was difficult to catch my breath. I closed the door to my car and followed Jake. As we approached the entrance to the house, I noticed the front door was old and had peeling paint. Anxiety of the unknown began to fill my mind and I began to have second thoughts.

Jake knocked.

Finally, after what felt like hours, a man came to the front door. His appearance was clean and he had a high-maintenance look about him. It looked like he had soaked his hair in hair spray for quite some time. I remember he was wearing a black shirt. He welcomed us in with open arms. *Hmm. That's odd. Dude doesn't even know me and he's already welcoming me in.*

The scenery within the home was rugged. Bedding sheets covered the windows. The paint was peeling off the walls. The lighting was low. It was as if the electric bill had been paid just enough that the lighting within the house could emit some sort of light.

The rest of the crew was in the dining room, surrounding the table, and playing a friendly card game. Jake's friend took him into the other room while I sat down awkwardly, viewing who had won the last hand in the card game. Everyone asked about me. They asked personal questions about who I was and where I hung out. I was oddly open with these people and they were oddly interested.

Finally, Jake and his friend came out of the back room. Jake seemed a little on edge. He immediately sat down and was dealt into the next hand.

Everyone smoked. It was like one big chimney in the middle of the dining room.

Jake's friend turned to me and finally asked, "So, where you from?"

I paused as though I could come up with some exciting famous city other than Joplin, but still I responded, "Joplin. Been here my whole life."

What? You couldn't think of anything better, Aaron? Everyone is watching and you come up with the same, small, boring town where everyone knows everybody? That's it. I have got to come up with some better answer than Joplin! How about Vegas? Yeah, Vegas. That's a gnarly place!

My thoughts kept my mind busy for a moment before I noticed everyone staring at me while I silently talked to myself.

Jake's friend replied, "Cool."

Cool? Oh, that's it, I was in! I was being accepted, not only by my fellow peers at school, but by the older, cooler crowd. As I was processing my awesomeness, Jake's friend pulled out a bag full of some sort of substance.

Jake immediately turned to his friend and said, "No! Don't give him that! He doesn't need that!"

Jake's friend completely shook him off and said, "You want a hit?"

Hit? Of what? I've never taken a hit of anything in my entire life, except for that one time I was hit by a baseball during a ball game. That didn't feel good. If I say no, he will think I'm a loser. If I say yes, I'm worried what will happen to me.

After a long period of hesitation, I said yes.

The baggie was filled with a white substance that was powerfully bright and transparent at the same time. The drug within the bag reminded me of a chandelier, one you might see in an upscale home or five-star dining restaurant. It was beautiful. It drew me in the minute I laid eyes on it. The substance? Crystal methamphetamine. I had heard of this drug before, yet didn't know anyone who had been on it or witnessed anyone ingesting it.

Jake's friend laid out a line of this beautiful substance on a handheld mirror and handed me a plastic drinking straw that had been cut off at the tip.

I willingly placed the straw within my right nostril. Lowering my head to the mirror holding the line, I saw my reflection as I swooped my head across the mirror and snorted as hard as I could. All I remember is the intensity of the burn. It felt as though I had just snorted a pile of broken glass. It was painful, unfulfilling, and unpleasant. I couldn't believe what I had just done. I felt full of shame and regret, but I reacted too soon. The sounds around me became clearer, as though I was encapsulated inside of a car full of subwoofers. The lights were brilliant, like bright lights you see from an oncoming vehicle in the night. Looking directly at the light almost blinded me. My mouth began to move at a rapid rate and my flights of ideas were spontaneous. I was thinking clearer and deeper, and, let me tell you, I felt better than I had ever felt before. I felt alive!

Immediately, I reached for a whole pack of cigarettes. I wasn't a smoker, but I picked them up as though I was an avid chain smoker. I smoked one cigarette after another, all the way to the filter. I didn't even acknowledge what I was doing. Then I found myself running to the bathroom in a panic. I fell into the toilet and vomited profusely until I had nothing left in my stomach. Then, I dry heaved even more. I felt dizzy and unbalanced, like I was going to pass out. Afterward, I stood up and looked at myself in the mirror—I had bloodshot eyes and tears were running down my face from the severity of my vomiting episode.

What had I just done? I don't smoke. Man, I feel sick. Won't be doing that again. I need to brush myself off and go back out there as though nothing happened.

I went back out to the dining area where everyone was sitting.

"You alright?" Jake asked.

I nodded my head yes and sat back down to join the card game. I felt great! I was having sensations I had never experienced before. Even my strategic card playing was professional. My mind was open and alert to new ideas I hadn't even thought of before. My mind was renewed. This was a great night. This was what I had been looking for. What I didn't realize was that I was experiencing a new world with a very dark side just waiting to devour me whole.

I knew it was morning when I saw the daylight seeping through the blinds.

Everyone went their separate ways and the night ended. Well, I *thought* the night had ended, but it really just carried on into the next day. I hadn't slept, not even a wink, but I wasn't tired. I was still alert and ready—ready to take on the next day and my next fix.

Since I had worked for about a year at my job, I had saved a little money to help get me by.

Jake wanted to continue our high, so he asked if I would buy another bag.

Without hesitation, we went to the closest ATM and pulled out another twenty-five dollars so we could continue this great ride!

Thank goodness it was the weekend and I didn't have school that next day because I could have found myself in an uncomfortable predicament. I had told my parents I was staying at Jake's mother's house that weekend, so I didn't have to face my parents on no sleep, not to mention high on drugs. So our journey continued that first weekend of my experience with meth and it was just the beginning of what would eventually become my nightmare.

That weekend was one of the best weekends I had ever had. I met new friends, stayed out all night, and had some really deep conversations about life. The weekend finally ended and my sophomore year was back in session.

Everything was going smoothly and I was reflecting on all my great memories with great friends, but my behavior was changing. I was becoming more irritable and moody. Other friends started noticing, and they mentioned it to me a couple of times, but I just brushed it off like nothing was wrong. I was at one point in my schooling an A+ student, and now found myself barely passing. My parents started noticing my grades were falling and wanted me to seek some tutoring, but I told them I would bring my grades back up to par. I was oblivious to everything collapsing around me. My social life was on fire, but my academic work was going down the drain.

My parents and I started fighting. Sometimes they were small fights about not doing my chores and staying out late. Other fights were horrendous, blowing up like the government had ignited a nuclear bomb in the center of our house. I was defiant. I didn't listen to authority. What happened to their well-behaved child? I was changing, and I didn't let anyone tell me otherwise.

One night, after my parents and I had a huge argument, I decided I wasn't taking this anymore and I would leave the nest. I didn't need my parents telling me what to do or how to run my life, so I chose to live my life outside my parents. I ran away. I made my way to my friend Craig's house, carrying only a few clothes on my back and some hygiene supplies. Craig and I had recently become good friends and had experimented with meth together and that's exactly what I intended to do this night—use meth as a getaway from life.

Craig lived in his mother's basement. We had everything we needed— a fridge, extra bedding, and a large supply of dope. We had been using consistently for about two hours when we heard a knock at the door to the basement. I wasn't about to answer that door.

We sat there in silence, but before we could even get up out of our seats, we saw two people in uniforms walking down the stairs. It was the police, and they told Craig they were searching for a runaway named Aaron. I sat quietly, knowing they were there for me, but there was nothing I could do. They picked me out based on a picture my parents had given them. *Traitors!* My parents had called the police and instructed them to visit Craig's house where they knew I would be.

The police slapped the handcuffs around my wrists and guided me to their vehicle. Police lights were flashing in the distance. I felt betrayed by my own parents. I knew this was going to put a huge damper on my relationship with them.

The police had taken me to juvenile detention hall for holding. I felt like a prisoner. I had been snitched on by my own parents and placed in a cell to rot away. The anger flooded my mind. I could think of nothing but hateful thoughts toward my parents. The detention officers made me strip out of my clothes and into an orange suit. As I was walking in orange toward my cell, I passed by other cell blocks. Each solid metal door contained a small window carved into the top. The men behind the doors were chanting like an army of men waiting for my hanging. Some were screaming bloody murder while others were taunting me. They wanted a piece of my hide. If they could have reached through the door and attacked me they would have, but the officers protected me by slamming my cell door shut behind me.

The room was pitch black. In it was nothing but a bed and a toilet. The screaming continued long into the night, and I felt as though my life was flashing before my eyes. This was it. I was going to spend my days in here as a criminal and I hadn't committed any crime. Well, I *did* run away from my parents, but I didn't see any harm in living on my own and being independent. I was beyond aggravated by the young men's voices as they continued spewing their vulgar words and hateful speech. I did what any boy would do when his flight or fight instinct kicked in, I shouted back even louder. The anger was apparent in my voice. They knew they had gotten to me. The young men started laughing at my anger, which increased my rage. I finally gave up. What point was it yelling and wasting my energy on a bunch of losers, anyway? I decided to give up and try to get some sleep. The threats and yelling went on throughout the night as my eyes became heavier, and finally I fell asleep as the background of voices diminished into silence.

I woke up the next morning and felt like I had the biggest hangover of my life—like I had been hit by an oncoming car. I knew it was morning because they had the lights turned on in my cell. I heard footsteps draw closer to my cell and the door opened.

"Mr. Garcia," the officer said. "Your parents are here to release you on bond."

I stood up and walked with the officer to the change station. After signing a few documents, they released me out into the lobby where my parents were waiting anxiously for me. I didn't even look them in the eyes. I had decided I wouldn't say one word to either of them because of the betrayal I was feeling.

They got the hint.

We walked separately toward the car and drove away as I focused my eyes on that awful place through the back window.

I began feeling more defiant, not only toward my parents, but toward any authority. In school, my grades kept failing. I skipped class with friends. I talked back to my parents. My life was beginning to fall apart. Piece by piece, my world was crumbling into a pile of dust that no longer had shape or form.

I started smoking cigarettes and experimenting with other drugs. Meth was my drug of choice, but I also started using marijuana, cocaine, and hallucinogens. Everyone knew my new hangout crew was completely consumed by drugs. Although I was popular with my classmates, I was beginning to be separated as a "drug head." I was okay with that. It was who I was. I didn't hide it or cover it up, not with my peers, anyway. My parents were oblivious to my drug use. They just assumed I was another defiant kid who was going through a phase. A phase…if they had only known I was developing a lifestyle that would eventually completely consume my life.

As the months went on, my sophomore year came to an end. I was about to transition into my junior year and I wasn't even ready for it. My grades had diminished and I was struggling to keep a sober mind. I found myself going from using on just the weekends to using every other day. I would use meth during the day in the bathrooms, the parking lot, and anywhere I could seclude myself to get my next fix. I would go to bed at night and lie in my room, acting as though I was asleep, when really, I was still high and suffering from drug-induced insomnia. I couldn't wait until the sun shone through the large window in my bedroom so I could get up, head back to school, and begin consuming again. Man, was I a consumer.

2

Stuck Between A Rock
And A Hard Place

The bell had just rung to signal the end of fifth period. As the students grabbed their bags and headed into the hallways, they began to stampede like a heard of buffalo. Two thousand students went to our high school, which was equivalent to the number of passengers on a large cruise ship. It was beyond crowded at our high school, yet left a lot of room for rumors.

High school was like one big, dramatic, gossip institution. Truth was non-existent within these walls, but for some reason the rumors never stopped. They only continued and caused what would be a huge threat.

The Columbine shooting had just occurred and it was all over the news. It was such a tragedy to see students rampaging through the school, killing and torturing young, innocent students with no remorse. That day, everyone at our school was talking about a student who was going to attempt a bomb threat on May 5th. It passed from one student to another. I began hearing about this threat more often until it was the only thing everyone was talking about. The teachers, counselors, and principals all became very concerned about this threat and weren't taking it lightly. But what could they do? It was merely a rumor.

The next morning started like any other day. I gathered with my closest friends and skipped class like it was another typical, defiant day. We had gone to a friend's house where we started smoking marijuana. I smoked joint after joint before I found myself in a trance and detached from reality once again. This was nothing new. I had known about this feeling before because I was forming a habit of drug use. I was accustomed to escaping reality by using drugs and falling in and out of a drug-induced coma.

After getting high, my friends and I contemplated what we would do for the rest of the day. When nothing came to mind, we decided to head back to school.

We arrived at school during second period. It was my study hall class, so as you would guess, we didn't do anything but get caught up in our other subjects. Not me; this was an opportunity for me to get caught up on sleep and fixate on my next high.

COINCIDENCE OR GOD?

I was day-dreaming when a fellow student brought in a pink slip from the principal's office. I knew this slip had my name written all over it.

The teacher called me to the front and I knew I was going to have to make a routine visit to the principal's office.

I slowly stood up and made my way to the front.

I knew they wanted to speak to me about skipping class again. I anticipated it and would gladly and willingly accept my punishment. I made my way into the hallway. It was surprisingly quiet and empty. I made my way around the corner toward the principal's office on what seemed like the longest journey down a valley of no return, but something seemed off. It felt like this was no normal meeting. I turned the corner and focused my eyes toward the principal's office through the glass windows and everything started moving in slow motion.

As I glanced through the glass, I saw a scene I had never witnessed before. The entire place was full of detectives, cops, and men in suits. It was as if the Joplin Police Department had set up shop in the middle of the school. I had no idea what was about to happen. With trepidation setting in, I opened the door and made my way into the establishment. As I walked through the door, the men began to set up a barrier surrounding me, almost like a squad of football players coming together for the huddle. They closed the door behind me as I made my way toward the principal's office, where I found my own mother sitting in a chair next to his desk.

What is going on? Why is my mother here? Why are there so many officers surrounding me? Had I caused this ruckus?

My mother was sitting there in a rage, with piercing eyes and her arms crossed over her chest. Her foot was stomping the ground. She couldn't believe the situation I was in and it was painted all over her face.

I was in complete shock. My eyes panned across from my mother and then focused on the principal, Dr. Kennedy.

"Aaron, have a seat," he said.

Confused, I sat down as he began to speak to me.

"Do you recall anything you did yesterday?" Dr. Kennedy asked.

Yesterday? I thought I was here for skipping class? Yesterday, yesterday... What happened yesterday? I went to class, got high, and headed home. Am I here because of the drugs? Am I in trouble for using?

As I went over the day in my thoughts, it hit me. It felt like a wall of shame bounced off my chest. I finally realized what I had done.

Dr. Kennedy saw it all over my face. "Yes. Do you remember making a bomb threat yesterday?" he asked.

I felt fear and shame all at the same time. I had completely forgotten that during sixth period I had written on a desk, "I will blow up the school on May 5th."

"It was just a joke!" I pleaded. "I wasn't going to blow the school up. I was just kidding. I had heard in the hallways that someone was going to do it, not me!"

Everyone around me looked away and began shaking their heads with disappointment.

My mother was ashamed because she, too, looked away and was almost in tears.

What have I done? How could I be so stupid? Why hadn't I erased it? What was going to happen to me now?

I had done it. I had written in pencil a threat to my school—that I was going to attempt to blow the school up—and I did it at the worst time imaginable. Granted, I had intended to erase it, but I was too high to remember to do anything like that.

Dr. Kennedy looked at me and said something I will never forget. "Aaron, you're stuck between a rock and a hard place right now." The police force, he told me, wanted to make an example of me. Because of the recent shooting, they weren't going to be lenient.

During the conversation, the prosecuting attorney made his way into the office and told me they wanted to put me in a correctional facility for two years as a punishment for my threat.

29

I can't go to jail. I'm just a kid. I'm not a criminal. You can't put me away with all those other offenders! What if I don't make it out alive?

My life was over. I was going away, once again, and I would be confined to an empty cell.

As I began to soak everything in, they stood me up and handcuffed me. I couldn't do anything but look over at my disappointed mother, who was weeping in the corner. At that moment, I felt sorry I had even stepped foot into this world.

What happened to her obedient son? I have let everyone down and now I'm going away for a very long time. If only I had erased that stupid message I wouldn't be in this situation.

The police surrounded me and escorted me out into the hallway. I thought I must have resembled a serial killer who was headed down the hallway toward death row. Something occurred that I never thought in a million years would happen: the bell rang and every student stepped out into my embarrassing situation.

Students surrounded me as I was guided out the door.

"Aaron, Aaron, what's going on?"

"What happened?"

"Why are you handcuffed?"

I kept hearing these questions from my peers as I made my way toward the exit doors. I held my head down in disgust and now know why convicted criminals hang their heads low. I resembled every person you see on television who has ever been thrust in front of the public eye after committing a crime.

They placed me in an all-white van. As if things weren't bad enough, I was being put into a correctional vehicle like I already resembled a convicted criminal. They knew I was going to be made into an example and wanted to physically demonstrate the consequences to everyone watching.

As the van headed down the highway, I could think of nothing other than how to escape. Escape? You would think I'd focus on how much I hurt my mother, or that I needed to straighten my life up, or how I was going to pay for a lawyer. Nope. I was focused on that door handle inside the vehicle and strategizing about how I could escape.

We finally made it to the city jail. I stepped out of the vehicle in shackles which they'd placed on me in the van, and made my way to the back entrance. I was booked for a bomb threat and placed in an orange suit. I experienced déjà vu, bringing me back to when I had been put in orange for being a runaway. It's never a good feeling being confined to a nine-by-six jail cell with a steel bed and toilet. You start to see how your life can be so easily taken from you. My life, I saw, was going in the wrong direction and I was becoming a professional criminal.

I spent two weeks in that cell. The only time I was able to come out was to make a statement about my view of what happened that day. I received no personal phone calls, no visits, and especially no privileges.

It was going to cost me. My lawyer said it would take ten thousand dollars to represent me because of the work it was going to take to plead my innocence. I didn't think of the magnitude of the money at the time because all I cared about was getting out. I wanted my freedom back, and whatever it was going to cost, I was sure I could figure out a way to pay it back.

My school had already suspended me for three months while I sat in jail. The teachers were willing to let me do my school work while I was on my suspension, but school work was the last thing on my mind. My focus was my freedom.

After two weeks and multiple statements later, they let me out on bond. My parents had helped me out by paying the ten percent to a bail bondsman.

While I was out on bond, I had to walk a straight line. I wasn't able to visit any of my friends. I found myself grounded from my car. The only activity I was allowed to do was complete the school work I had missed. It wasn't much, but I lay low while I was out of jail.

After one month, the prosecuting attorney and judge finally came to a verdict—two years of supervised probation, one hundred and eighty hours of community service, and the two weeks I had spent in jail while I waited on a decision regarding what they were going to do with me was counted as time served. On top of that, I was unable to go back to school for another three months because I was placed on suspension immediately after I was arrested, which prevented me from hanging with friends and using drugs.

I was relieved I didn't receive the two years in prison. I was let go with a misdemeanor verbal assault charge that wouldn't be on my adult criminal record. Man, was I released by the skin of my teeth. Do you suppose someone was on my side?

This was a point in my life when I came to a fork in the road. Either I was going to change my life and make a full recovery, or I was going to continue using drugs and hanging with the wrong crowd, which would be devastating for me. Not only did people now see me as a threat, but they noticed everything falling apart in my life. My parents didn't trust me, my friends didn't know who I was, and now I was on the radar of the authorities. Which would I choose: the narrow path leading to a good life, or the wide path leading to destruction? I had to make a clear, conscious, sober decision.

3

Auditory and Visual Hallucinations

It had been three months since I stepped foot onto high school grounds. For the past twelve weeks, all I had focused on was my bedroom door. It's not very encouraging sitting at home when you're suspended from school. You would think I enjoyed being involuntarily expelled from school, but my patience was wearing thin. Now that I knew I was prison-free, the addictions started coming back. My idle hands began to fidget, and my thoughts were consumed with getting high again.

I had no idea what to expect on the day I was allowed back onto school grounds. I kept thinking about what my image would be now. Was I identified as a criminal or a man with a plan? I opened the door to school that day and instead of a bad experience, I got a sweet surprise.

The minute I walked onto the mats of the foyer at school, everyone approached me.

"Aaron, you're out!"

"Man, it's good to see you."

"What a surprise to even see you back in school."

All these responses were surprising. Instead of being frowned upon by my peers for my absurd behavior, I was being acknowledged as a celebrity.

Is this really happening right now?

All morning, students and close friends surrounded me and gave me their attention. I soaked it in like a sponge. I was like a freshly opened Christmas present no kid could resist.

On the flip side of the coin, teachers, counselors, and other authorities kept their eyes on me and followed me around like hungry dogs, not that I paid any attention to them. I felt, at this point, bulletproof.

After the first week of school and my increased popularity, things seemed to calm down and everyone went back to normal.

Jake had graduated and moved on.

I insinuated myself into other formed groups.

I was seventeen years old and had been clean for over three months. I felt like my old self again. My *new* high was feeding off attention.

I ran into a very unique group of individuals. They were younger than me, but they caught my eye. Well, the girls in the group caught my eye. The leader of the group was a young man named Trey. Trey was a confident, suave young man who had many women surrounding him. Trey was a good looking guy; he kind of resembled Denzel Washington. Once I got to know him, I found *he* even had some eccentric acting skills that would fool his own mother into letting him do anything. Trey was a drug addict, like much of my generation at Joplin High, but he kept his composure well. Trey's drug of choice was marijuana. This guy could smoke a field of swag and go to school displaying no evidence of being high. He could even provoke any young woman to submit to him, literally. He was an upcoming, popular guy in whom everyone saw potential.

Trey and I became good friends. We had a lot in common. Well, we had drugs in common, which does not make a healthy relationship. Every weekend we would get together with groups of girls and party. I found myself back in the same patterns as before I had been arrested. I was smoking marijuana and doing dope once again, but this round of people introduced me to another awfully strange substance.

Trey asked me if I had ever "tripped."

Tripped? Like awkwardly fell over onto my face and got back up feeling embarrassed? Sure have. That doesn't sound like some kind of exciting high to me.

Trey began to talk about a drug which took you out of reality and caused you to hallucinate. He described it as the greatest high ever. The drug, which is also known as "acid," "trip," "sugar cube," or "LSD," was a drug most teenagers didn't mess with, but I was open to anything because I loved exploring new things.

Trey got the acid from a dealer who lived in a local apartment complex near Missouri Southern State University. Trey was the only one who was allowed to communicate with this mysterious man. I would drive him to a spot around the corner from the apartment complex and he would run up to the dealer's door, alone.

When you wait for drugs, it's an overwhelming, anxious experience. I call it the "waiting game." Sometimes you come back with the jackpot, whereas other times you come back empty-handed. You never know the outcome when dealing with drugs; you just roll with the punches. Sometimes you get more than what you expected.

On one trip, I waited for almost thirty minutes before Trey finally approached my vehicle and got in. He had two sugar cubes wrapped in foil. One was extremely large compared to the other. He glanced over at me with wide eyes. "Dude, we got more than we paid for!" Trey shouted.

"What do you mean we got more than we paid for?" I replied.

"My dealer accidently dumped the rest of the bottle on one of these sugar cubes."

Seriously? Could I have been any more ignorant?

Acid in Joplin then ran about five dollars per drop, and each drop is equivalent to a Visine drop. We usually bought two drops at a time to get us by. Not knowing the amount of acid on this sugar cube was terrifying.

Trey and I had come to a dilemma. Would Trey be the one to ingest the saturated sugar cube, or would it be me who took it and possibly didn't come back to reality? This was a tough decision.

Trey said he didn't want to take it because he didn't want to be "up" all night. Acid has chemicals in it that create insomnia, and if you take too much it can keep you up all night, just like meth.

I was more scared than nervous. I mean, I had taken acid plenty of times, but no more than two hits at a time. This sugar cube could have had forty hits in it and I wouldn't be able to tell. All I could tell was I was in for a crazy ride.

I had decided to take the sugar cube despite my hesitant thoughts and unclear mindset. What was I thinking taking this many hits? Was I basically asking for the worst case scenario with the craziest outcome?

Trey handed me the drug and I opened the foil. I looked at it. It looked just like it had all the other times I had taken it—a white sugar cube like one you might place in your coffee cup. I paused. No, I *really* paused, as though I was waiting for the gun to go off at a track meet. Then I placed it in my mouth and took in the flavor. I knew once the sugar cube dissolved immediately in my mouth it was *saturated* in acid because most of the time it took about two minutes to dissolve. This was going to be really bad.

How could you be so stupid? You really just took in a drug that could kill you with that much or even put you on a trip detached from reality for life?

I wanted to vomit. I wanted all of it out of my system.

I was scared for my life because I didn't know what was to come next.

After taking our acid, we drove off and picked up the girls.

Shay, Tonya, and Andrea all got into the car and knew we had just ingested some trip. It wasn't their first rodeo. They had been with us before when we hallucinated, but it hadn't been like tonight. Tonight was going to be one eventful night. They usually just made fun of us as they sat in the back seat, gossiping about other students at school. We would be lost in translation and they would be lost in everyone's business.

About thirty minutes passed and we pulled into the parking lot of a Mexican restaurant.

The girls loved smoking marijuana and knew Trey always carried some. The drugs hadn't kicked in yet, but when they do it catches you off guard. So, as Trey was rolling a blunt, I scanned back and forth across the parking lot, waiting for something to jump out at me.

Finally, Trey lit up the blunt and the smoke filled my entire car. If you've never heard of "hot boxing," it's the way to get the highest off your product. We rolled up all the windows in my car and didn't roll them down until the entire blunt was smoked. There was a haze over the inside of my vehicle. I could no longer see the restaurant in front of me. I went into a trance and everyone laughed while Trey and I anticipated the arrival of our high. When you smoke marijuana with the acid, it intensifies the high. You get more out of your high than what you usually expect.

We finally finished the blunt and decided to get out of the car. It was blazing so much in the car that I couldn't find the door handle to get out. I blindly moved my hand back and forth across the door, hoping to catch it, and when I did, I ripped it open. I looked back after I got out of the car and saw my car go up in smoke. It almost appeared my vehicle was on fire, but there wasn't a flame, just a marijuana cloud.

I was severely high. My eyes were almost completely closed.

The girls were falling over laughing at Trey and me. We were starting to feel acid.

I became extremely hungry. We call them the "munchies" after smoking, and I was focused on immediately going into the restaurant to place an order. Why I would go into a restaurant after smoking a blunt and swallowing a vial of acid was beyond me. I didn't care; I was hungry and on a mission.

Shay went with me.

The rest stayed behind and smoked a cigarette outside my car as Shay and I made our way toward the front door.

I wasn't even nervous. I was so hungry that all my thoughts were left aside.

As we came to the front door, I opened it and a gust of wind blew directly over my body as though I was on top of a skyscraper in the windy city. I almost lost my balance when the wind hit me, but I caught myself and proceeded forward.

When I walked into the restaurant, I couldn't even focus because the lights were so blinding. I knew the acid was setting in. Everybody appeared to me as though they were out of some cartoon movie. I found myself laughing uncontrollably, like someone set me inside of an enclosed chamber and filled it with laughing gas.

Everyone was staring at me at this point.

I started drawing unneeded attention, was exposing my goofy self, but I didn't care. I was having a good time.

I tried to make my order at the desk, but I couldn't collect my words together. It came out sounding like I was speaking a foreign language.

The teller couldn't get my order right because I wasn't making any sense, so Shay had to place my order for me.

We had sat down with our food and I devoured it like it was my last meal; I don't think I even chewed the food. I was dazed by all the lights and colors I was seeing at that moment. The air smelled fresh, the colors were satisfying, and my mind was like mush. I took in all the great auditory and visual hallucinations, which I thought were real at the time.

Suddenly, something changed. My thoughts started to race, the intensity of everyone's voices caused me to cover my ears, and panic was consuming my mind. I immediately got up.

"What are you doing? Are you okay?" Shay asked.

"We have to get out of here. We need to leave now!" I shouted.

Shay didn't know what was going to happen next, but she knew I was beyond my own capabilities and directed me out of the restaurant.

I could barely walk. My equilibrium was completely thrown off and I felt handicapped. I was almost crawling out the front door.

When I got out of the restaurant, the visual hallucinations became more intense. I focused on the parking lot. Parts of the cement opened up and vines grew out of the ground. One after another, these vines grew into trees all around me and I freaked. The parking lot was turning into a jungle. Bushes grew and covered the restaurant and my mind was taking me out of reality. I found the closest bush I could and jumped into it. While I was in the bush, trying to hide myself from everyone, there was nothing but fear within me. I was shaking, paranoid the jungle was going to eat me. When my panic continued to grow, I visualized Native Americans with spears, stabbing me over and over again. My screams became louder. I couldn't keep my terror within my body. Those Indians were actually my friends trying to get me out of the bushes and take me to safety, but I was so high I assumed they were trying to kill me.

Finally, the group saved me and threw me into the car. They placed me in the passenger seat and attempted to calm me down. It was working. They put on some nice, slow, good-feeling music to help bring my mind peace. I'll never forget the song that played: U2's *I Still Haven't Found What I'm looking For.*

Have you ever caught yourself in a moment when you tried finding what you were looking for? I immediately started wondering if I had found what I was looking for. Was I still looking for acceptance? Was I still searching for something greater? In that very moment, I hit a breaking point in my life and decided I was running out of control. I needed to slow down or else I was going to find myself beyond repair.

COINCIDENCE OR GOD?

As I listened to the music, I focused on the jungle covering the city. I saw the beautiful greenery and color of everything around me. I saw monkeys swinging from vines, and other exotic animals. I was out of my mind. I had replaced the reality I lived in with a fantasy.

After twelve hours of tripping, I finally came back to reality and fell asleep.

The next morning, I awakened and my neck was completely stiff, like I had slept on it all night. I felt like utter hell. Last night was a night I would never forget and today I was feeling the effects.

I will never again take something so strong that I have no control. Thank God I didn't die or lose myself forever.

I decided I was living life too wildly. I made a choice to place drugs on the back burner for now and finish school out right. My grades were beyond low and I had to really buckle down if I wanted to finish my senior year. I did what I had to do. I attended every class and brought up my grades. I graduated high school by the skin of my teeth. Everyone thought I was graduating with my diploma in general studies, but what I really walked away with was a degree in narcoticology

4
The Devil's Den

May 22, 2000—the day of graduation—had finally come. I had been preparing for this day for the past three months. I had ordered the cap and gown, had my senior pictures done, and had passed all my subjects. I had finally done it. Looking back, I could have changed some things, like maybe not running into the wrong crowd, making poor choices about threatening to blow up schools, not giving in to temptation, and maybe even obeying my parents, but here I was, finally done with high school.

I barely passed and had used up all the days you could miss, but I didn't care, I had done it! Four-hundred and fifty students graduated with my class, which was filled with future teachers, lawyers, doctors, and, of course, drug addicts. This was the year of "Y2K." You remember, don't you? This was the year 2000, when the conspiracy rumors spread regarding all the computers shutting down across

America and preventing anyone from accessing their bank accounts, personal records, or retirement investments. The whole country was in a panic and preparing for the worst. We were the graduating class attached to that conspiracy.

Obviously, you know none of that happened. Instead, we graduates would use this year to reflect on all our accomplishments. It's such a surreal experience when you graduate high school. Your family is so proud of you; you have developed relationships with other students and made memories to last a lifetime. My memories, no matter how crazy they were, were good.

We got ready in the gymnasium next to the graduation auditorium. Flashes of cameras blinded me. The students were crowded together in a small area. I could barely hear myself think with all the chatter going on around me. Laughter, excitement, and joy filled the room.

It was time. The students filed toward the auditorium in a single line. We made sure our caps were level and our gowns were zipped. Then the doors to the auditorium opened up and I walked through the bright light. The coliseum was packed full of parents, teachers, and family members, as though we were some sort of professional sports team making our introduction. It's a different level when you walk into a crowd of onlookers who are there to witness your graduation. Can you remember your graduation day? It's a chapter in your life that is hard to forget. This memory in my life still comes back to me from time to time.

As we took our seats, the principals and administrators began their speeches. I can't even recall what they said because I was in a state of complete serenity. I clapped when everyone else did and whooped and hollered along with everyone as well. I saw my parents in the distance, waving and flashing their cameras. I just laughed and awkwardly waved back.

When it was all said and done, they made us all stand. As we moved our tassels from the right to the left I knew it was finished. We had done it! Everyone's caps filled the air, and in a movement that felt like it happened in slow motion, we all leaped for joy. Like swells on the ocean, my classmates' bodies moved back and forth. Tears and hugs flowed contagiously throughout the room.

My family and I went home to continue the celebration. My parents had a party all ready for me at the house. Taking countless pictures with family and friends took up most of the night, and, of course, the gifts came as well. I don't know about you, but if I could graduate once a year that would be great! I received thousands of dollars and gifts filled my room.

Why can't this happen every year?

But the night soon ended and everyone went their separate ways.

Reality hit the next morning. I woke up to a graduate breakfast, which I'd like to call your last meal of no responsibility.

My parents asked the question I had been fearing, "So, I guess it's time to get a job and move out on your own?"

What? Get a job? Move out? Oh, man... I'm not ready for all this. I'm not ready to grow up yet. I'm ready to hang with friends and continue living lavishly.

For those who don't know, graduation in my household means getting a job and becoming independent. At least, that was my parents' suggestion. I started by looking in the daily newspaper—nothing. I moved into the bedroom where the computer was and browsed the internet—nothing. Everyone wanted applicants to have a college degree or some sort of experience. Me? I was a high school graduate who was at the bottom of my class. I was the bottom of the barrel and the last among the crowd. This was a difficult realization. I had no job and didn't have any ambition of going back to school, at least, not at that time.

I finally had to consider getting a job in the food industry. It wasn't like I was going to be there long, but I had to prove to my parents I could hold a job and move out on my own.

My partying continued. I hung with people with whom I probably shouldn't have been hanging.

In the midst of working my part time job and partying during my free time, I ran into a young man named John. John was a fit young man with a black belt in karate and competed in mixed martial arts fighting. He was a tall, stout guy—not someone I would mess with. But he had a kind heart and seemed genuine. John was like no one I had met before in my crazy life.

John and I bonded immediately. He enjoyed talking with me and cracking jokes, and I saw him as a bodyguard. It wasn't like I needed any protection, but in such a situation, John would have my back.

John invited me over to his house, and one day I had some time to go over. I pulled up to the address he had given me. It wasn't in a bad area; it was even on a busy, main road. John lived in a duplex with his mother, his sister, and her boyfriend.

I rang the doorbell and John's sister answered the door. Terry was John's older sister. She was blond and slim. She was very inviting and told me John was downstairs in his room.

The stairs to John's room were immediately to the left when you walked through the door. At the bottom of the steps was a closed door. I knocked lightly and heard a shout, "Come in!" I opened the door and made my way in.

I'll never forget the first time I laid eyes on John's room. The furniture was all black leather, the walls were old and wooden, and the carpet was dark red. It resembled a place where the devil would reside. I called this room "the devil's den," and I couldn't have been more correct.

I figured before entering John's room for the first time that it would be calm and collected. Nope! John's room was filled with men blow-torching glass meth pipes and beautiful women snorting meth off glass mirrors while John stood in the background.

"Come here, Aaron" John said.

As I walked across the room toward John, I passed all the addicts sucking on their pipes and people snorting lines off the coffee table.

"Welcome," John continued. "I'm glad you came." John introduced me to all of his friends.

Although I was a recreational meth user, I had stepped into a new place of uncharted waters. I had stepped into a realm so deep that the dark waters could have swallowed me whole. But I felt right at home, and once again fell back into my habits as I took the line of meth offered to me.

John and I talked all night—laughing, sharing stories, and becoming close friends. All in one night, I met new people, did more than my fair share of dope, and fell into a dark place where most people would never go. By the end of the night, which was now morning, John asked me if I wanted to move in and split the rent downstairs. It didn't cost much to live there and my parents obviously wanted me to live independently, so I agreed to moving in and helping pay the rent.

My parents had no idea what their son was stepping into; they were just excited to see me becoming a man by living independently. They had no idea I was about to move into a drug house and become completely subjected to drugs. I never even put two and two together. I was excited to be starting a new chapter of my life. This chapter, however, would be the destruction of my life.

I packed all my things into my car. I no longer drove the Toyota Tercel because I had moved on to better things. I now drove an Acura Integra with a black finish and black leather interior. It was a sweet ride. I had used the money I made from selling my Toyota and my parents had covered the rest using what was supposed to be my college tuition. I was a stud, or so I thought, driving a sick ride and living independently.

Since the devil's den was downstairs in the basement, the only window in the entire room was a small, sealed window you couldn't even climb out of in case of a fire. The living room was the main area and had a bar in the back corner and a bathroom behind it. The basement had only one bedroom, so I mainly slept on the couch, when I was *able* to sleep. Okay, let's be honest, we didn't sleep. How could you sleep when your nose was full of dope? But the bedroom was there in case one of us needed to crash.

Upstairs there were two other bedrooms where John's mother and sister slept. Terry, John's sister, was an alcoholic. She drank with her boyfriend daily. During the day she would sleep and at night they would hit the bars. Late at night, I could always tell when they were home because the amount of banging upstairs was unbearable. Joanne, John's mother, was a single parent. John's father had left the home quite some time before, and it wasn't something we talked about much. The kitchen and living room were upstairs as well, but we had basically all we needed downstairs.

My part time job didn't last long. I was so distracted by getting high that I didn't have time to work. My recreational use of meth went from using on the weekends, to every other day, to every day. It was every day, I tell you. It didn't stop.

John had an unlimited supply of drugs he got from meth dealers.

I never understood how John had so much dope. He didn't work, and yet he always had some with him. So I popped the question, "John, how do you get your dope?"

"Easy," he said. "I make it."

Make it? Like actually create it? How do you make meth? Do you use kitchen ingredients? That's crazy!

At night, John started teaching me about how to cook meth. He taught me all the ingredients poured into this strong substance. He even wanted to introduce me to some high-ranking cooks. I can't remember if what I felt was the drugs flooding my brain or the actual excitement of creating something with my own two hands. John also told me about the power and control that came with cooking meth. John had women around him all the time, and people awaited his every move. He could ask anything of anyone and it would be done. Yes, John had authority in the city of Joplin and he was taking me with him.

John had connections to high-ranking people all around Joplin. John introduced me to a group of individuals—a family of drug dealers. The chief in command of the group was Brian. Brian was a quiet individual who didn't let anyone into his circle. Can you blame the guy? I mean, he was one of the most powerful drug dealers in the city of Joplin. Brian's cousin, Mike, was his right hand man. He was more outgoing, so he was the one who did all the talking. Brian and Mike were a team with one thing on their mind—meth.

The cousins allowed me in only because they trusted John. They were quite standoffish at first, but we all became really good friends. I was the jokester of the group; I could make anyone laugh by being goofy. Outside of our small circle, there were groups of people that attached themselves to us. We had some of the purest drugs in the city and never cut any of our product. In fact, we would make our product even stronger. We found ways to increase our batch.

We called it "work." Just like at any other nine-to-five job, we worked every day of the week. We found ways to get the ingredients and when we did, we would go to work. We were developing a reputation, but we didn't allow anyone to get close to us. If some of our outside friends wanted to introduce us to other people, we would decline the offer. If we were going continue to stay under the radar and produce some of the most powerful substances, then we had to stay secluded and let no one in. If people wanted what we had, they would have to go through one of our servants. We had power beyond our wildest dreams; we had authority to make anyone do anything we said. We were at the top and there was no one who could stop us.

Drugs used to be a fun form of social interaction, but drugs were taking over my entire life. I didn't even see it coming. Well, let me elaborate: I didn't see it coming to *this*. I figured we were just young men enjoying life and living it to the fullest. Oh, how wrong I was from the start.

I developed a circle of friends whom I called family, but the only way we were related was through meth. I would scan my phone and all I would see were addicts, dealers, and cooks. Not one of them was living a sober lifestyle. The only contacts I had who were anywhere *close* to sober were my parents.

How disappointed they would be with me if they knew I was a drug dealer and manufacturer.

By the way, do you want to know how I paid for food and rent? Dope. John's mother was also a drug addict. What were the chances, right? I moved into a home where the son wasn't the only addict in the household—the whole place was full of addicts.

We went to work as usual and made all sorts of different batches. Typically, we would end up with about fifteen hundred dollars worth of dope, and my share was about five hundred dollars. It was plenty because in about another three days, we would repeat the sequence again. I would hand over a couple grams of dope to John's mother a month, and that didn't include the complimentary lines we gave her throughout the day as a generous token.

What was even worse than feeding John's mother with dope was we were dealing drugs to single mothers who had children to feed and who would instead spend all their money on drugs. I'm not proud of it, but the only things on your mind when you're high are power and money, and I had both. My morals and beliefs went out the door when it came to meth. We were considered sorcerers—men who were making the devil's potion and destroying people's lives.

I didn't realize the person I was becoming by allowing drugs to control my life. What happened to the young boy my parents raised up? Did he become lost in the world? Would he ever come out alive? Even if he did, would he know who he was? What used to be fun was becoming the darkest place of my life. It was the deepest abyss into which one could sink and the most unfamiliar road to the point of no return.

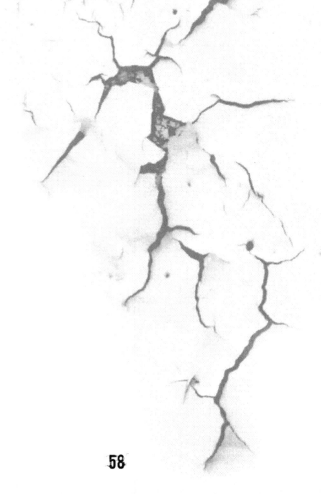

5

Fear

It had been two weeks since I had slept. Meth is a stimulant, so it keeps you awake throughout the night, and I had done so much dope I hadn't slept in weeks. Can you imagine not sleeping, even for one night? Sleep deprivation can do some funny things to you, and it can also lead to paranoia.

Tonight we were headed to the country to make a huge batch. We needed to be completely secluded from society if we were going to be careful about making meth.

We hooked up with Brian's uncle, who owned a two story house out in the country. We were setting up for a big night.

Brian had gone ahead of John and me and taken his mobile meth lab with him. Imagine all the instruments and supplies used in a chemistry class set up in one vehicle. It was dangerous. Luckily, we wouldn't be carrying any product in case we got pulled over by the police. We were always so careful about moving labs from one house to another.

My job when it came to cooking was that of the "dishwasher." My duty was to clean the meth lab up once the cooks were finished, and I was rewarded very well for my services.

We were all set up and ready to go. As the dope was being cooked, there were a select few who were permitted to be present. There were three women, who were friends of Brian's uncle, John, Mike, and me.

The fumes filled the air in the basement where we were cooking. Although I was high already from snorting a pile of meth earlier, the fumes were more potent, so I was maxed out. We call it "spun out." It's kind of a funny way of putting it because my mind was literally spinning. I was focused on Brian and Mike, who were cooking up a storm. Literally, a wave of evilness was occurring in the middle of the room, and then it happened... I felt a sudden, uncomfortable feeling. I went into a panic. I went from being uncomfortable to being terrified. "They're here, they're here!" I yelled. "Quick, we have to get out of here."

Everyone turned to look at me as I yelled out obscenities.

"What do you mean they're here?" Brian asked.

"The police," I yelled. "They're outside, I just know it."

They all looked back at each other and rolled their eyes, thinking this guy is either crazy or he is frightfully right.

"You're just tripping," Mike said. "Sit down and shut up."

I sat down quietly, but couldn't hold it in. "I have to get out of here," I continued. I began to pace around the room and peek out each window. I looked between each blind because I figured I could get a better view of what was outside.

Finally, Brian told a girl named Sharon to get me out of there and take me home.

I grabbed my coat and handed her the keys because I wasn't in any condition to drive. I slowly opened the back door and we made our way to the front where my car was parked. I didn't see any cop cars in the area, but still assumed they were near. We got into the car and slowly drove away. I kept my head down and underneath my coat. My mind was racing a million miles an hour.

We pulled up to a local truck stop in town because Sharon had to get something to drink.

Is she setting me up? Why are we stopping?

I glanced over the dash and watched men and women walk in front of our car. All of them were watching me, I just knew it. I thought *surely* they were undercover cops waiting to arrest me. They had gone inside the truck stop and Sharon was still inside.

Are they planning a setup?

61

As I was freaking out, Sharon walked outside to the car, got in, and we drove off.

I watched her as she was driving.

Her eyes panned from the rearview mirror back to the driver side window.

"What are you doing?" I questioned her.

"Nothing," she replied.

I told her to take me home and I would give her money for a taxi.

She agreed and parked in front of my house.

I jumped out and ran downstairs where I thought I would be safe. Right after I settled myself in the devil's den, everyone showed up and surrounded me.

"What's going on?" I spoke.

"Nothing. What's going on with *you* is the question," John said.

Brian, Mike, John, and other dope heads kept questioning me about why I had acted so crazy back at the house. They said I risked them getting caught by the cops. They were not happy with me.

I started to assume they believed *I* was an undercover informant. "You guys don't think I did this on purpose, do you?"

They didn't know what to believe, so they all left to continue their binge and sell their dope. Me? I took a couple of sleeping pills and laid my head to rest.

The next morning I awoke from my sleeping pill slumber. The dope I had earned from the night before was lying on my bedside table. At this point in my addiction, I couldn't even get out of bed until I had snorted a line of dope. I finished my morning breakfast of meth and went back into my paranoia. No longer was I having fun with the drug, but the drug was having fun with me. Every time I snorted more dope I became more paranoid and confused. It came to the point that I didn't trust anyone, not even my parents. I was sure everyone was out to get me. My fear of being caught by the police or being killed by high-end drug dealers would be the downfall of me.

Today was my grandmother's birthday, my parents had invited me over for a get together with family. The whole family was there, from my grandmother to Aunt Lucille, to my first and second cousins. When the party migrated to the living room, I made my way to the bedroom to watch television alone. I hadn't slept in days. My mind was racing with paranoid thoughts, and voices began to speak within. I heard my family gossiping about me in the living room, or so I thought. Everything started building up inside of me and I couldn't take it anymore. It was almost as if I was breaking out of an insane asylum in my head. I slammed the door open and stormed out of the room.

I screamed into the living room, "You're all against me!"

There was a moment of deafening silence and then everyone's eyes were fixed on me. It was so embarrassing to have my whole family looking at me as I accused them of something they had no idea about. I turned to the front door and made my way to the streets. It was bitterly cold outside, but I didn't care. All I thought about was how to escape and never come back.

My father ran after me out the front door and walked with me at a fast pace.

"I'm never coming back, do you hear me, Dad? Never!" I yelled. I had convinced myself that this would probably be the last moment my father and I were going to have together.

My father broke. He began to weep, and the weeping turned to sobbing. "Please, son, just tell me where you're going," he said. "I just want to know where you are so I can check on you."

That hit home for me. I had broken my own father. The man I had looked up to my entire life was now sobbing at the very thought of losing his son. I felt terrible. I felt bad that I was hurting my own family and hadn't even known it until this moment. How could I hurt my own father? How could I say such mean things to a man who had cared for me since my birth?

"Well, can I at least give you a ride home?" my father asked.

Without even thinking, I said, "Yes." We had a very good talk about life all the way back home.

My addiction wasn't just on the surface anymore. My addiction was at the very center of my life. As for all my morals and conscience, they were gone. My hopes and dreams were shattered. My future and goals had vanished. I was becoming a walking, talking zombie with no soul and I couldn't even see it with my own two eyes. My family and peers saw I was losing my life to drugs and turning invisible. I was surrendering my life to a substance completely designed by the devil.

Cooking meth used to be exciting. It used to make me feel powerful. I could manipulate anyone into doing anything, but now I visualized something different. I was seeing it for what it really was— sorcery. The devil was using it to destroy families, neighborhoods, and communities. And I was seeing it firsthand. You would think that once I discerned the evilness of it, it would divert me in the other direction, but on the contrary, it sucked me in deeper.

I was climbing the dope tower and moving my way up the ranks. Brian no longer saw me as a "dishwasher," but as a wingman in his army. Brian and I drew closer and started cutting everyone else out of the group. We would secretly go and cook meth alone, which left more product for us. I was now raking in thousands of dollars of meth a week. Talk about a rush. But I was falling deeper and deeper into psychosis at the same time.

Brian and I hooked up with a connection in town, where we felt good about setting up shop. It was a small, brick house, but nevertheless, it was perfect for quick in-and-out access. The owner of the house didn't want to be present during the cooking, but wanted her portion of the finished product. I'll never forget the visual I got on this night.

Brian had set up and we were ready for work. As the chemicals were combining, and after the reaction had taken place, we placed the cleansed product into a pan on the stove.

I stood back as the final phase was occurring. I lay on the couch and witnessed something I had never seen before. The fumes of the potion Brian was finishing up began to seep through the room. Patterns started developing in the white substance filling the air. What I thought was just smoke pouring into the room was forming into shadows on the walls. Once chatter. "I've got to go, got to go!" I shouted.

Brian looked back and just shook his head, "Not again. Sit down and shut up."

"No, no, no," I said. "We've got to get out of here. There are demons all around me."

All of a sudden, Brian didn't appear to be Brian anymore. His face was blackened and I could no longer see his face through all the smoke consuming him.

I tried to make a break for the door, but came up unsuccessful because all the deadbolts were locked and I didn't have the key. I raced down the hallway to find another way out—nothing. All the rooms were locked as well. The walls began to shake as I made my way back up the hallway to the kitchen where the sorcery was going on. "Run, run, run!" I shouted. "We will surely die here."

Brian grabbed me, threw me on the couch, and handed me a glass pipe. It was almost like when you give a baby a bottle to calm him down. I lit the lighter and started sucking on my pipe and everything seemed normal again.

As Brian finished the batch, he handed me my share and we scurried out the door, back into the streets.

Brian told me to drive and I complied with his wishes. I was still trying to soak in what had happened at that house. I was overwhelmed with anxiety and more than my usual share of paranoia.

He told me to pull up in a certain driveway. It wasn't a place I had been before. This was new. Well, the house was old and looked like it could fall over any minute, but it was the first time I had been here.

"I'll be right back," Brian said. "Don't get out of the car."

Brian had made his way into the house and I cranked the radio up so I could get lost in my music. Minutes passed and nothing happened. I continued to listen to Creed in my car and wait for Brian's return. Then the door opened. What was supposed to be Brian was not him, but a posse of five men storming out that front door and surrounding me like a pack of savage wolves. The fury in their piercing eyes told me that they meant business. Their pants were torn and they were wearing nothing but wife beaters. Every one of them had a shaved head. They almost looked like they had walked out of their own concentration camp. As they continued to surround my car, I noticed they had something else that gave them an advantage—Louisville Sluggers. Each of them had one. They hadn't come to ask me to join their baseball league; they had come to kill me.

I immediately turned my stereo off and locked the doors.

"Come out, come out where ever you are," they shouted. "We won't hurt you. We just want to play." They started chanting and shouting like a bunch of hyenas prior to their kill.

One of the men approached my window and slowly tapped on the windshield. "Get out of the car," he said.

You would assume I would beg for mercy, but my reaction wasn't a symbol of surrender, mine was the middle finger. "Get lost," I shouted. Man, thinking back, I should have negotiated a little better, but when my fight or flight kicked in, I couldn't help but get aggressive.

The men stepped back and got into a position much like that of Mickey Mantle in the batter's box. They were preparing to charge my vehicle. I was on the brink of death and I didn't say one prayer. I just sat there, welcomed my fate, and gave up.

Right before they charged, Brian came running out the front door. "He's with me," he yelled. "He's with me, stop."

The men all looked back at him, confused.

"He's with me," Brian said. "He's not a cop."

This whole time these men had thought I was an informant and I had stepped foot onto one of the biggest dope houses in Joplin. It was the big house, the center of the map, the point of no return, and Brian was there selling some of the best dope in Joplin.

Brian got into the car and we drove off.

"What the hell happened back there?" I shouted.

"Sorry, man," Brian said. "I didn't know they were going out there."

"Well it sure as hell scared the crap out of me," I said. "I thought I was a goner."

"I know, I know. My bad," Brian said.

We drove off into the night and once again pushed everything aside and started consuming.

Fear was no longer something that occurred once in a great while, fear was every day and everywhere. Fear was being in my car and believing someone was in my back seat. Fear was believing the cops were always following me. Fear was seeing demon-possessed people all around me. Fear was hearing demonic chatter penetrating my mind. Fear was losing my grasp of reality and falling into the dimensions of hell. Fear was all I knew.

I was a "window watcher." I would constantly look through the blinds and wait for something to happen. I looked across the street from the upstairs living room at a white van. I knew, just knew, that it was the cops and they were about to invade our home.

"I have got to get out of here," I told John. I grabbed my things and decided to head to my parents' house. I opened the garage door and made my way to the main street. I was suspicious. Looking back at that van, I didn't see it move, but I knew there were other undercover police vehicles following me. I adjusted my rearview mirror and watched for any unmarked vehicles. Every time I looked in the mirror I assumed it was a police officer following me. I put my foot on the gas and sped up. I made my way quickly to my parents' house and pulled into the driveway. I thought, at this point, the police had to have placed a tracker under my car, so I got out and looked underneath. I tweaked out on the under carriage of my vehicle. I looked in between the cracks, pipes, and muffler. I reached in between all the clutter and came up short. I couldn't find anything resembling a tracker.

My mother heard me outside and came out to the garage. "What are you doing?" she asked.

"There's a tracker under here, Mother," I said, "and I am going to find it."

"You are on drugs!" my mother shouted. She made her way back to the garage door and slammed it.

After who knows how long of searching for the tracker or some sort of detective device, I came up short. I found nothing.

I made my way into the house for shelter, and ran into my old room, closing the door. I immediately went to the large window in my room and looked through the blinds. I saw that same white van parked in a neighbor's driveway across the street. At least I *thought* it was the same white van. It could have just

71

been another white van, but I was too high to grasp that concept.

My mother asked me if I wanted to go to the antique mall with her. There was no question in my mind, I wasn't going to stay here and be with the police. I eagerly accepted her offer.

We arrived at the antique mall parking lot. At this point I didn't know who to trust, not even my own mother.

Is she setting me up? Is this part of the plan to take me to jail?

We made our way into the mall and began bargain shopping. Not me, though; I was cop supervising. I was waiting for someone who looked like an undercover cop. I couldn't tell who was who because they all looked the same. Because of my disorganized thoughts, I suspected everyone in the building was a cop.

I knew what I was going to do. Instead of them watching over me and playing games, I was going to steal an item to *make them* take me to jail.

Yeah, that will fix them alright.

I grabbed an old military hat and made my way to the front. It appeared the people around me were getting ready to make a move, so I threw down the hat and awaited our collision. Nothing happened. Surely they were going to arrest me after I had stolen something off the shelf, but they didn't.

Mother was checking out at the cashier and I was standing back to back with her. It reminded me of a war movie in which two soldiers lay in a bunker, back to back, anticipating a strike from the enemy. I started hearing choppers over the building.

Are they getting ready for a huge sting operation involving helicopters? Surely I'm not that much of a threat. Is the government involved now?

Mom purchased her items and we made our way out the door. When we got out the door, the skies were as blue as the ocean. And wouldn't you know it, nothing was in the sky and not a cop was in sight. Let's just say the mind can play some funny games. But was this a game I was playing or was this real life? And was this real life going in the right direction or in a direction in which fear and psychosis would lead me straight into a psych ward? Only time would tell.

6.

Revelation

My mind was a battlefield—a playing ground for the devil to come and enjoy tormenting me and controlling my thoughts. My hands and feet were attached to strings manipulated by the dark one who played me like a puppet. I have to admit I was losing my grasp on reality. I admit I was losing the image of myself I once saw in the mirror. I have to admit I had gone further and deeper into a sea of forgetfulness than I had ever sank before.

My life, which was consumed by meth, was absent from reality and I was fighting my own demons. I had opened a portal to a realm which can't be seen with the naked eye. An area of darkness and pain I was enduring from drugs. A sea of lost souls where I was absent from my life. I felt nothing but utter terror as I witnessed the fear before me. Only through my addiction could I see we were at war in the spiritual realm. Not one heart was pure. Not one spirit was alive. The images I was seeing were like arrows penetrating into the depths of my soul.

Because of my addiction, I felt trapped inside my brain, almost like being within a psych ward, restrained by a strait jacket. I was screaming out for help. I had lost fifty pounds of fat and muscle. My cheeks were sunken in and the bags under my eyes were like grand canyons. I was a walking corpse—a pile of bones. My face was covered with sores and bruises from my compulsive picking. Spending hours in front of the mirror, I obsessed over the landscape of my face. I picked and prodded deeper and deeper until there was nothing left of it. I wanted to peel the skin off my face so I could see the undercarriage of myself. I was sick—deathly ill by the drug that was once my entertainment. Now my entertainment was watching men and women picking through the carpet for hours in a panic, looking for their dope. My entertainment was watching sorcery being manufactured without conscience. My life was no longer a gift, but my worst nightmare. It was a place I could never have imagined and wouldn't wish on my worst enemy.

I made several attempts to commit myself into a psychological facility for a consult, but someone always kept me from getting help. I wanted out, but the friends I had surrounded myself with were all consumed by meth. The only two people who were anywhere close to being sober were my own parents, and I had already lost that relationship. They knew now that their son was a dope head because of all the events that unfolded. Oh, you know, like tweaking under your car for a tracker the so-called cops had placed, or freaking out on your entire family during your grandmother's birthday.

I found myself at rock bottom—the lowest I had ever been in my entire life—and I wanted out. I wanted a bus ticket to the nearest somewhere— somewhere other than this life. I wanted to be anywhere but this place. And here I was in the devil's den, by myself, with nowhere to go.

I found myself at the bottom of the stairs and feeling pain so real I could literally feel the weight of it on my back. It felt like I was squatting and holding the world on my shoulders. And something happened—something unimaginable—something I had never felt before.

What I'm about to share with you is no coincidence, but a miracle. I needed help. I couldn't do it on my own. No, I needed something supernatural. The only place I knew to look was up, so I focused my eyes on the ceiling of that dark, gloomy place and experienced a revelation. With my eyes full of tears, to the point that if I had blinked it would have soaked the carpet, I spoke, "God, if you're there, I need you. I don't want this life anymore. Please, save me from this dark place!" I yelled, in complete surrender. After sobbing to the point of exhaustion, I trudged to bed.

To this day, I can't recall the next three days, but it was three days. It was like I walked in my sleep through those next seventy-two hours and woke up face to face with my roommate, who was screaming violently at me.

"Get out! Get out!" John raged.

I couldn't understand what was going on. For no apparent reason, I was being kicked out of my own house. I wept. I had no words to conjure up while I packed my bags. "I have nowhere to go," I sobbed.

"I don't care," John said. "I want you out of this house now."

I picked up my bags and headed toward the front door.

Everyone had their eyes on me with a look on their faces that said, "take care of yourself."

I exited the front door.

Where am I going to go? What will I do? Am I going to sleep on the streets?

I found myself in a huge predicament. I would either have to build up the confidence to drive to my parents' or find a box in an alley 'til daybreak. Something inside me told me to head to my parents'. I knew I would find shelter there.

I stood in the dark and rang the doorbell at my parents' house.

My father answered the door. "Come in, Son," he said.

I walked in, hesitantly, with my head down and sat my strung out self on the couch. "I need to talk to you guys," I said. "I was wondering if you guys would allow me to stay here for a while?"

The intensity in my mother's eyes was like I remembered from when I was in the principal's office getting handcuffed by the police. It wasn't a pretty sight.

My mother had anger and tears in her eyes.

My father was standing in the background, looking at me with sympathy as though he felt sorry for what he was witnessing.

The person my parents saw before them was a man with no soul. I had been told many times that my sclera, which is the white part of the eyes for you non-clinical individuals, were completely black. Some spiritual professionals refer to black sclera as an indication that the individual has no soul. My parents couldn't believe they were witnessing their sick son in the condition I was in. What used to be their son was an underweight, malnourished, strung out, lost boy who desperately needed love.

My mother was so scared for what her son had become that she opposed me moving back in.

My father, who was always there for me even though he was afraid, said, "Well, he's our son. We can't just kick him back onto the streets."

What seemed like the longest pause in history was the hope I needed for my life to go on.

"Okay," my mother said, "but only if you stay under our roof and get clean."

I unquestionably said, "Yes!"

The next three days were not a walk in the park. The severe withdrawals came. My parents had made sure to keep me safe and locked in the house. I slept. No, I mean a sleep resembling that of sleeping beauty, except without the mushy love story. This was bitter hell. I experienced body aches, night terrors, profuse sweating, and hibernation. I only woke up to use the restroom and drink the water my parents brought to my bedside.

The window was blacked out for my comfort. I couldn't get enough blankets to keep my body warm. Then, after three days of rest, I awakened, but to a sobering perception of reality.

If I was going to beat this addiction, I knew I had to make the ultimate sacrifice—I had to shut my phone off completely. Every contact I had in my phone was an addict, except for my parents, of course. And I was with them, so there was no use in having it anymore. I had a dozen missed phone calls and more than twenty text messages. I didn't even read them. I was burning my old life and moving forward with a purpose, so I destroyed my phone, completely. Do you remember that scene in the movie *Office Space* when they take the printer out to a field and smash it to smithereens? That was me. I broke my phone into a thousand pieces and I felt alive. Okay, not really. It was the hardest decision I had ever made, but I knew it was the right one.

Then came the second phase of withdrawals: reality. I was so used to being high that I forgot who I was. This was a major problem. I didn't know how to act in public. I had forgotten how to be funny, how to interact, and most of all, I had no idea who Aaron was anymore. This pain brought anxiety and depression into my life. Have you ever hit a point in your life when you felt like you'd lost yourself? It's a life-changing moment, that's for sure.

My parents suggested getting a prescription for antidepressants, but I had to press forward with my life, and that meant *no* drugs. I needed a job if I was going to get myself out of this depressed state of mind, so I decided to go back to being a line cook in a restaurant. It wasn't much, but I needed to start somewhere. I got a job at a local barbeque restaurant. Boy, did I stink. I came home filthy, covered in smoke-injected pig and cow hide. My shoes were always covered in so much grease I was embarrassed to bring them inside my parents' house.

Is this what life is all about? Coming home just to take your third shower of the day?

It wasn't for me. I knew my life was meant for so much more.

I was watching television during the middle of the day.

Mom was home for her usual lunch break. She could tell I wasn't happy but I was being obedient to staying sober. "Hi, honey," my mother said softly. "How is your day off?"

"Fine, I guess," I said.

"Hey listen," my mom said. "I was thinking, have you ever thought about going into the medical field?"

I turned the television off to make sure I had heard correctly.

"No, not really," I answered.

"There's an ad in the newspaper about a phlebotomy class."

I stopped and pondered. "Hmm…I could give it a shot."

Once I decided to pursue it, things moved quickly. I got into the phlebotomy class. For those who don't know what a phlebotomist is, the best definition would be that we're vampires. No, we're not really walkers of the night who sink their teeth into humans. I mean we draw blood from people's veins. *Phlebo* means vein and *tomy* means incision into vein with a needle. Got it? Alright, I'm moving on.

After the six month program was over, I received my certificate. Back to cloud nine I went.

My parents were proud, and I was surprisingly proud of myself. Now, where was I going to get a job? I hoped I would get a job with one of the clinics where I had done my internship, but they didn't have any open positions.

As I was browsing through the paper one day, I came across an ad for a local plasma center which was looking for an experienced phlebotomist. I was no expert, but I thought it wouldn't hurt to apply.

I met with the manager after filling out my application.

"You got any experience?" she asked.

"No, not really," I replied.

There was a long pause. She just stared back at me as though something had caught her eye. "Hmm…When can you start?"

Today! Today! Give me some scrubs and I'll head out to the floor now!

I had to keep my composure. "As soon as possible," I replied so softly.

"Okay, come in early next week and we'll get you a badge and start orientation."

If I could have done anything I would have leaped into the air like Judd Nelson does at the end of *The Breakfast Club* and remained stuck there while the credits rolled across the screen, but I kept my composure and shook her hand. "Thank you so much for the opportunity," I said. I exited the center with one confident, *Jersey Shore* fist pump. I had done it.

I eagerly looked forward to my first day at the local plasma center. I was eager to see what favor would fall. I was eager to start this new chapter of my life. Shoot, I was just eager to have a good job. Okay, I was more than eager, I was anxious.

The job was fast-paced and located in a plaza full of donors and medical personnel. As a phlebotomist, I would stick people with a needle hooked to a plasmapheresis machine and monitor for reactions. I fell in love with it. I thought it was a great job with great opportunities. There was a lot of advancement and promotion to be had, but one of the jobs that caught my eye was that of those dang nurses. I'm not talking about them being eye candy like most of you are probably thinking right now. Yeah, I saw your thoughts churning. No, they attracted me with their *compassion*.

I couldn't contain the curiosity. I had to approach one of them. Well, when I mean approach one, I mean I approached a pack of them. "Hey, guys."

"Oh, hey, Aaron," one of the nurses replied.

"I've got a question for you," I said.

"Sure, go ahead," the nurse replied.

How am I going to ask this? Um, how do you...? What is it...? Where can...?

I couldn't decide how I was going to ask the question, so without any more hesitation, I asked, "What does a nurse do?"

They all smiled at each other as though I had asked one of the stupidest questions in clinical existence. "Aaron, we save lives and help people," one of the nurses said. "It is the greatest, most rewarding career you could possibly get into."

Holy crap. That is awesome. Such a reward? Such compassion? It seems like I have hit the jackpot and I haven't put any pennies into the slot machine yet. That's what I want to do. I want to reach out and help people in a time of need when they feel vulnerable. I want to go to the ends of the earth and save the sickest people.

This was what I had been waiting for my entire life.

I ran home to my parents like I had just received a golden ticket to Willy Wonka's chocolate factory. I busted open the door, but luckily the hinges were still intact. "Mother, Father!" I shouted. I found them in the dining room, rounding up bills. "I know what I want to be. I want to be a NURSE."

They jumped up with such excitement I'm pretty sure our utility bill went down the vent, but who cares, I had found my calling.

We sat there and spoke about my future and the great new chapter in my life. We laughed, we cried, we shared stories, and we hugged 'til the sun set. This was what God had called me to do. He had been molding me this entire time, until he shaped me in the right image, and now he was giving me ambition to take on a new task. This next chapter of my life is what I like to call *opportunity*.

7

Foley Catheters And Cadavers

I opened the letter I had long awaited. As I broke through the seal and unfolded the stationery, I held my breath.

"Dear Aaron, We are excited to announce that you have been accepted into Missouri Southern State University."

My eyes filled with tears. Although I was hit with other emotions—excitement and adrenaline—I couldn't hold back the tears. I was accepted into college.

It was such a surreal experience stepping foot onto college grounds. I had gone from a local high school to a gigantic university. It was mind blowing to see myself going through a period in which I engaged in destructive behavior, then turning my life around and earning a college degree, from narcotic abuse to advanced chemistry, and here I was smelling the sweetness of opportunity. It *is* the American dream after all, isn't it?

In high school, students have classes five days a week, but in college? I had class maybe three days a week. Could it be any easier? Of course not. I understood I had two years to achieve above average grades if I wanted to get into the nursing program. I also had to earn a twenty on my ACT in order to get into nursing school and gather good references. I had to buckle down and take the wheel if I was to be in complete control of my destiny.

Things were looking up. My relationship with God was beginning. I found my prayer life increasing, and it helped give me strength to go on through my daily struggles. I was never great at school, but would find myself praying to God to give me wisdom through it all. I will admit, I'd never really had a prayer life. I was always so independent before, but now I was seeing God everywhere and I wanted Him involved in everything.

I was still living a crazy life. I had switched meth for alcohol.

As long as I stay away from the hard drugs, what could it hurt?

But what I was doing was surrounding myself with a different crowd. I was a non-traditional student, which meant I was older than most students, but I continued my child-like ways.

I hit the bars routinely and experienced nights of chasing women and blacking out. I wish I could remember a lot of what went on during those nights, but I can't seem to pull many memories up. It's scary, huh? I was going to class hungover probably two of the three days I had school per week. I suffered through my first classes, and then, come the afternoon, I was ready to hit the clubs again.

I'm what you call a polysubstance abuser—I trade one addiction for the next. But it wasn't the alcohol I was addicted to; it was the lifestyle that came with it. Everyone and their mother drank. It was marketed all over the television, on billboards, and down the aisles at the local grocery store. What harm could it bring, really?

One night, I went on a binge that lasted well into the night. A friend and I had been consuming alcohol for hours and decided to hit the club. After multiple shots and beers at the club, we had to stumble to the car and drive home. As we were pulling down my street and close to the driveway, flashing lights blinded me from behind. I don't recall much of the evening, but was told the police walked up to the vehicle, and after they opened the door, I fell out into the street. I was intoxicated. My blood alcohol level was over three times the legal limit, the officers told me.

What is wrong with me? I could have been killed.

What was worse about the incident was that my own parents and grandmother woke up to the flashing lights in front of the house and came out to witness me being placed in handcuffs and hauled off to jail.

After sobering up, I found myself walking out of the city jail and slapped with DWI charges. Once again, my parents gave me a ride home. It was déjà vu. I knew I had a problem with alcohol and needed to stay out of the club scene for a while if I was going to get anywhere in college.

Two years passed, and I finished my prerequisites. I had a 3.5 GPA and had done very well in all my classes. I never knew the potential I had. Where was all of it while I was in high school? Oh yeah, I know, I was too focused on dope. It was quite an awakening to see my brain work the way it does. I had been out of school for five years and had been scared I couldn't complete college, but since the brain is a muscle, it only took a bit of work to get my brain back into the habit of studying.

I was ready to apply for nursing school, but there was one thing I was lacking—my ACT. Since nursing school was only accepting letters for two more weeks, I had to focus on taking my ACT and scoring at least a twenty to have a chance at being accepted. I was never a good test-taker, especially when it came to an accumulated exam gauging my strengths in different subjects. Luckily, there was one more ACT class open to students before the year ended. I signed up and had two days to study for the exam.

When I opened the ACT review booklet, it was like reading Chinese.

Seriously? How am I going to pass this exam? I can't even absorb what they are telling me.

I couldn't think about all the difficulty ahead of me. I had to buckle down and just do it. The exam lasted three hours. Three hours! My mind was like butter.

I waited for my results from the ACT exam. Did I ever tell you I hate the waiting game? It was like waiting on death row, if I could imagine what that waiting would feel like. But the envelope finally came two days later. I opened the envelope with sweat pouring down my face and skimmed through all the babbling, "Thank you for your interest in the ACT exam," and so forth. I panned down to the bottom of the letter. Can you guess what number I received on the test? Yep, a TWENTY. I busted out laughing, as though it was set up this way.

I couldn't hesitate. I had to get all my information to the nursing program quickly. I placed all my information in the envelope, almost forgetting my return address because I was so excited, and sent it off to the post office for special delivery.

Six months passed and the nursing program finally sent out their notification letters. I received my letter, but I just stared at it for thirty minutes.

Just open it, silly. What are you waiting for?

Finally, I gathered my courage and opened the letter. This letter was the most important letter of my life at this point. Like a child on Christmas morning, I ripped the envelope in half. Luckily the letter was still intact. "Thank you for applying to the nursing program. We are thrilled about your future in the career of nursing. However, at this time, all positions have been filled, but you have been placed on the alternate list."

Wait a second…. The alternate list? I'm an alternate. That means I wasn't accepted? Read the letter again, Aaron. That can't be right.

I read it again. I was an alternate. When I think of an alternate, I think of the last of the bunch—a spectator, a person who is lower than average, a good for nothing. That's what I felt when I read I was an alternate in the program. My heart sank into my stomach.

How can this be? I did everything I was supposed to. My GPA was good, my ACT score was satisfactory. What is going on here?

I told the news to my parents, who felt my pain.

"There's always next year, honey," my mom said. "And who knows, you might still get in!"

Next year? But I wanted it now.

I couldn't believe what was going on. This was the first time I had felt real disappointment since getting clean, and let me tell you, it's one of the worst feelings ever.

After I got over my disappointment, I threw the letter away and went back to my job. Everyone at work asked about my news. They knew I had received the letter in the mail because it was the only thing I talked about. When I presented the news to them, they, too, were disappointed. I have to admit, I definitely had a good support system at the plasma center, but it still didn't make me feel any better about the situation.

It had been two weeks and I knew the nursing program was two days away from beginning. This was confirmation I had not gotten in. I was hurt. I thought everything was going to work out according to my plans, and when your plans don't come through you are left with disappointment. Have you ever felt like that in your life? It's not very pleasant.

I was working full time at the plasma center, which kept me from thinking too much about not getting into the nursing program. I went on break during one evening shift. Routinely, I went to the locker room to check my phone, and this time I found that I'd missed one call and had a new voicemail. *Hmm...* I checked my voicemail and it was a woman's voice.

"Hey, Aaron, it's Patricia from the nursing program. If you would, could you give me a call at your earliest convenience?"

That's odd. What would they need from me? Oh, I know, I probably forgot to fill something out on the application. I'll call her to give an update. It's no big deal.

I made the phone call in the middle of the locker room.

"Hello," a female voice answered.

"Yes, this is Aaron Garcia," I said. "I received a message from you guys?"

"Oh yes, Aaron, I left the message," she said. "How are you?"

"I'm good. Did I forget to write something down on my application?"

"No, everything is perfectly fine," she stated. "Listen, Aaron, I was calling because there has been a change."

A change?

"One of the nursing applicants who was accepted…. Well, she backed out and will no longer be attending our program," the woman said.

I was confused. "Okay."

"Aaron, we were calling to ask you if you would be interested in joining the nursing program."

I could not believe what I was hearing. I let it sink in.

"Aaron, are you still there?"

I hadn't realized I was in shock and hadn't even responded. "YES, YES, YESSSSS! I would love to come be a part of the nursing program," I shouted over the phone.

She laughed. "Great. We are excited about your new adventure."

I ran around the locker room thanking God for this opportunity. The words came rolling out. "Thank you, God. Thank you, God." This was new for me. I was praising God right in the middle of the locker room and there was not a soul around to witness it.

I ran back out onto the floor and told everyone the good news. "I got in. I got in. Everyone, I'm going into the nursing program."

My coworkers all turned, grinning from ear to ear, to congratulate me. There were tears of joy and happiness, and I couldn't believe how blessed I was. Now, all I had to do was get a physical, pass a drug test, and get closing signatures, and I had to do it in two days. This was my next problem, and I didn't have a lot of time to get it completed.

I still was in shock from the phone call confirming my spot on the team, but in my mind I was like the athlete who says, "Put me in, coach. I'm ready!" I had to focus on getting everything done in a timely manner or I was going to miss my opportunity. Physical? Check. Signed documents? Done. Drug test… Oh, come on. I was drug-free and feeling great about life. I finished everything according to their requirements and was granted access into the wonderful world of nursing.

We gathered in the auditorium the first day of school. The dean and instructors introduced themselves and the program syllabus, which gave us an idea of what to expect. Let's just say it wasn't a peaceful experience. I thought this was going to be a joyous occasion, but instead, it was a clinical boot camp set up to intimidate even the strongest candidate.

I'll never forget the words, "Kiss your spouses and children goodbye because for the next two years, you're ours."

What? Kiss them goodbye? I'm not being shipped away to some deserted island, am I?

This was not what I had signed up for. I thought that we were going to study about how glorious it was to be a nurse and the impact we would have on the community.

Okay, I'm getting a little crazy about not learning what it meant to be nurses, because we did. I was just overwhelmed by the information and the massive amounts of work it was going to be to graduate from the program. I'd heard that a Bachelor of Science in Nursing is one of the most difficult degrees to obtain, but I thought it was just another bit of propaganda. Boy, was I in for a rude awakening.

Oh, and another thing, they never talked about the amount of stool, fermented urine, open wounds, and dead people you would encounter along the way. Seriously, I thought nursing was about keeping people comfortable and providing great care. I had no idea about the nasty, vile, potent stench that comes along with it.

Nevertheless, I was excited about beginning one of the greatest chapters of my life. I pushed everything else aside and told myself I would give it all I had. And all I had was myself to give.

We learned and studied everything from respiratory management to congestive heart failure, from blood-borne pathogens to blood pressures, from septic infections to diverticulitis. If you don't know what most of those are, that's okay—I recommend you Google them. That's what everyone else does, right? Look up everything on *WebMD*?

And another thing—they wanted us to stick objects in places I had no idea they could go. *You want me to stick that where?* I was becoming experienced in Foley catheters, nasogastric tubes, and a little thing called a Flexiseal, which is also known as a "butt plug." No one prepared us for the mental scarring that was taking place in our brains. We learned via "jump in and do it" instructions. That's how they introduced and taught us the ways of nursing.

It was the last semester of nursing school and my grades were way above par. They actually consisted of As and Bs, which I hadn't seen since before I got into drugs. I felt like a scholar. I was back on cloud nine. I felt like I could conquer the world, until I got a grade update from my instructors.

They had called a meeting between me and all of my instructors. "Aaron, come on in."

I closed the door behind me and took a seat in the only open seat available.

"Your grades aren't where we would like them," one instructor said.

I knew I had slacked that semester because I had contracted a little "Senioritis" and hadn't studied like I should have.

They proceeded with my grades and told me I would have to do everything in my power to improve them if I wanted to graduate. Actually, these were their exact words, "It would be almost impossible to pass this semester."

My heart dropped and the tears began to fill my eyelids. It was my own fault, but I had no idea my grades had dropped that low.

"I'm sorry to break the bad news," an instructor said, "but you will have to study intensively, and even that might not be enough."

I left the office and cried all the way home. All my hard work was shattered by that one office visit. I knew if I was going to do it, I would have to work harder than I had ever tried before, and I would need God to help get me through it.

Over the next few weeks, I buckled down. I mean I strapped myself into the seat and grabbed the wheel. I studied night and day. Sometimes I would study in between several hour chunks of sleep. On top of all that, I studied even more. I connected with one of the girls who was at the top of the class. She took me in and we studied all week. We covered the respiratory system, cardiovascular system, endocrine system, and even fluids and electrolytes. It was brutal. It was like my mind was a sponge someone had thrown up against the wall and left it to slide down into its own puddle of mush.

The day of the final arrived and I had done everything I could do. I had given it all I had and studied consistently until there was nothing left in me. The instructors told me I needed an 83% on the final, which was the hardest final of the program. I knew that not many students got that high of a grade. Actually, the instructors had to grade on a curve because the exam was so difficult. There was one more thing I was missing from this puzzle—my prayers and requests to God.

God, I'm in a bind here. I know I screwed up by slacking, but if you could help me out in any way, I would greatly appreciate it.

It was some powerful prayer, right? Let's just say I'm no professional at prayer, but it was all I could come up with. Nevertheless, I sat down and took my final. Let me just say this: it was the most intense, difficult test I had ever taken in my life, but I finished.

When the results came in, I breathed deeply, knowing the outcome would dictate my future. Without any further hesitation, I looked at my score. Can you guess what I got? I got 83%. When I looked at the score I began to weep and thank God for getting me through this difficult time. As I glanced at the score, I heard a voice in the back of my mind say, "I'm here with you, son." It was my first encounter with God which helped me realize that He is always with me. It was a life changing moment and it shifted my perspective forever.

I had successfully completed nursing school.

Graduating college was such a fulfilling experience. The auditorium was full of family and friends. The sight brought me back to my high school years, but with a more mature perspective.

My instructors couldn't help but smile back with tears in their eyes.

I chose my parents to pin me at the nursing ceremony. As they walked across the stage and met me in the middle, we cried and hugged.

The first words out of my mouth were, "I love you guys."

As a whole, all the nurses took an oath to always protect, honor, and care for the sick. We vowed to value being nurses and to never give up on ourselves. It was amazing. Actually, it was *more* than amazing, it was surreal. I had graduated college and couldn't believe how far God had brought me from the darkness. I was ready to start my career and take on new challenges. I was ready to help and care for others. I was ready, but I wasn't prepared for the encounter that came next. No one could be ready for what was about to happen to an entire city…

8

Organized Chaos

May 22nd, 2011 was a day just like any other. I awakened to the sound of my morning coffee brewing, to the brightness of the morning sun, and to another normal (or what I believed would be normal) day. I had been working in the ER at Freeman hospital for two years now and really enjoyed what I did. It was the second of two ER's in the city. I got ready, threw on my scrubs, and headed to work.

Driving in to work, I heard over the radio that thunderstorms were coming. It was no big deal; a little thunderstorm never hurt anyone.

I pulled into the parking lot and made my way through the emergency doors. Nothing was different about this day. I cared for the patients with different medical complaints, such as abdominal pains and fevers, just to name a few. I worked mid-shift, which happens to fall on the busiest times of the day.

All day long, people watched the news and prepared for what the newscasters were calling a pretty bad storm. Being in Missouri, we see a lot of unusual storms. Actually, storms were common and the norm here in Joplin, Missouri. So we continued our daily work and put the weather in the back of our minds.

We were joking in one of the nurses' pods when we heard over the television that large pieces of hail were beginning to fall and to take cover. I drove a 2010 Chevy Camaro and was not about to let my beautiful princess suffer any damage from the hail storm. I know what you're thinking, but my car was my most prized possession—it was what I took pride in. I decided to go outside and move my Camaro underneath the parking garage. When I walked outside, I noticed the sky was completely green and the air was so dense that the pressure was smashing my face. I thought it was very strange and I had never seen anything like it, but I continued what I had set out to do and parked my car in the garage. Then, I walked back in to work.

In the emergency department, there are no windows. There are only walls and patient rooms. I couldn't see what was going on outside. We heard the hail coming down by the sound of the pellets hitting the ceiling. The intermittent pinging soon turned into a shower of hail. It sounded like metal bullets trying to pierce the building.

It was 5:20pm and the lights in the entire building shut down.

What the heck? What just happened?

We were in complete darkness. After about ten minutes of being in the dark, the generators turned on and we got a small amount of electricity. It was barely enough to light the patients' rooms and our nursing station. The call light phones at the nurses' desk began to alarm. I couldn't shut them off, so I ended up gathering newspaper and covering the speakers to muffle the sound.

This is very strange.

I got up from the nursing pod and made my way out into the hallway. Looking around as though I was looking for something in particular, my gaze made its way down toward the waiting room doors. I heard a sound coming from the waiting room. Then, in an instant, the doors to the emergency room busted open! A fleet of men and women were running full speed right at me.

What is going on?

I couldn't believe what I was seeing. Men and women were covered with debris and blood and screaming bloody murder.

"Holy crap!" I shouted and looked back at the other nurses. Either there was a massive wreck or something really, really wrong had happened.

The swarm of people running right at me began to move to the sides of the hall as the triage nurse pushed a critical patient toward me. This man was holding his own intestines in his lap as his head bobbed back and forth. He was going in and out of consciousness.

"Aaron, we need a room," the nurse said.

I held my breath. I could not believe what I was witnessing. I just pointed toward the trauma bay doors. Then, I came back to reality and followed the patient to the trauma area.

We began to wrap the patient's belly to hold in the intestines and stuck a breathing tube down his throat to manage his airway. This guy needed emergent surgery.

"What's going on, everyone?" I shouted to all the healthcare staff in the room.

Everyone stopped and looked back at me, "We have no idea."

Then it happened. People began to bring bodies from everywhere around the city. The waiting room was no longer a waiting room, but an extension of the ER. Something terrible had happened to the city.

The flood of people swarmed the ER through the waiting room doors. Ambulances, trucks, and other unauthorized vehicles pulled up to the back doors. The best way I can describe it would be to imagine downtown New York City with no lights, no stop signs, and no caution. The people began to crash into one another. They brought body after body. This was not a normal day, but the result of a catastrophic disaster that had hit Joplin. This was organized chaos.

We found out that an EF5 tornado had hit the city of Joplin and we were at ground zero. We were told the hospital next door was completely demolished, so they started hauling their patients over in trucks. Some people were already dead, whereas others were in critical condition. People were being carried in on their own front doors for support. Others had 4 x 4 boards through their chest. Not one was in stable condition.

Charge nurses and physicians started directing patients to rooms, but the rooms began to fill up. Rooms that once were single patient rooms began to fill with more than ten live patients. The hallways, which were normally empty, were used as areas where people were laid down. Not any space went unused. The break room was now the suture room where we stitched up lacerations and wounds. The morgue looked like a salvage yard where bodies were dumped. We couldn't have prepared for this night. We hardly kept it together.

I was starting IVs in patients and giving pain medication with what short supply we had. The medication areas were locked when the power went out, so the pharmacists had to walk up to the emergency department and set up shop. They started handing out antibiotics and pain medicine. We were running out of gauze, knee braces, and supplies, so central supply had to continuously bring us more. Everything was out of order. Everything, I tell you! I saw men and women with bones sticking out of their skin. We just kept putting their legs back in place and moving on. There were times when I was intensively working, followed by exhaustion.

I looked over at other nurses and saw the fear in their eyes. These nurses had no idea if their own families were even alive. Phone towers were down and there was no cell phone service.

I asked every ambulance driver who came in, "23rd and Maiden Lane, is it gone?"

"Everything is gone, everything," they would shout back.

"What do you mean it's all gone?" I yelled back as I gripped their jackets.

"Aaron, it's gone," one said, "all of it."

Reality was sinking in. In the back of my mind, I knew my house was completely gone, but nonetheless, I had a job to do; I had to save lives. I got back to business and began wrapping people's wounds, giving pain medicine, and comforting them.

There were two phrases everyone was saying, "God, save me, God!" and "Where's my child?" It was terrifying to say the least, but I was called to serve the community, especially during a natural disaster.

Something began to shift in the ER. Nurses from all over the area started showing up and asking how they could help. I started designating them to different areas. Physicians dressed in civilian suits came to help, and ambulances from all over the region came to transport patients from the overfilled ER to different areas. The community was coming together and in a big way!

Through all the organized chaos, I could tell the atmosphere was changing. It was as though there was a peace, not just among the patients, but with the staff as well. Cell phones were coming back into service and people were able to reach their loved ones.

I checked my phone and found a message from my roommate, "Aaron, I'm sorry, but your house is gone. I'm here at my brother's house and I'm okay, but the house is demolished."

Even though I had known my house was probably gone, it couldn't take away from actual reality. I broke down. All I had worked for and owned was gone. Have you ever lost everything in your life? It's the most unimaginable feeling. It feels like your gut has been ripped out of your abdominal cavity.

2010 had been the best year of my life. I had gotten the job in the emergency department, moved into my new house, and was engaged to my then girlfriend. It was followed by the worst year of my life. My house was gone, the city I had grown up in was destroyed, and I lost my engagement due to unfaithfulness. I felt like life was coming down on me and I hadn't prepared for it.

As the night became morning, I looked around and knew there was nothing else I could do, so I went home after seventeen hours in the emergency department taking care of thousands of people.

I drove to what was supposed to be my home. I had to maneuver between electrical lines and debris, but I finally pulled my car into my driveway. It was pitch black in the city of Joplin, so I moved my headlights onto my house. It was gone, most of it. The pressure from the tornado had blown half of my house outward and shifted the foundation. I didn't dare go in to see what I could salvage because it was too dangerous. I left with tears in my eyes and drove to my parents' house.

When I arrived, my parents hugged me and told me how sorry they were.

I made my way to the extra bedroom and collapsed onto the bed. I was completely exhausted.

The next day, I had nothing better to do so I went in to work. As I walked back into ground zero, the entire place was empty. Rooms that had been filled with bodies and pain were now an evacuated emergency department. The smell of iron was strong in the air while housekeeping personnel were attempting to wash the blood off the walls.

Everyone was still in shock from the previous night. Counselors were making their way around the department to see if anyone needed therapy, which I declined at the time. I didn't know that over the next two weeks I would have flashing images of that terrifying night haunt my dreams.

The May 22nd tornado devastated Joplin and destroyed over eight thousand homes. The EF5 tornado was a mile in diameter and tore through the center of Joplin, covering fourteen miles with destruction. A high school was leveled, St. John's Hospital was destroyed, and many other business and families lost everything. One hundred and sixty three people lost their lives to the tornado. There are no words to say to those who lost, who were destroyed, and who are still rebuilding.

Although there was a lot of chaos, I want to share some goodness that came out of it. Thousands of people flooded Freeman Hospital that day, but only one percent died, and most of that percentage was people who were already dead when they came in. We had twenty-two emergent surgeries, and more than a thousand patients were cared for and discharged.

One nurse, Tracy, had been working that night in the ER and had taken a patient to the morgue. When she placed the patient in the morgue, she looked over at a child who had been black tagged and left for dead. She thought it was her own son, but it wasn't. She walked over to him to get a closer look, and when she did something miraculous happened: the boy opened one of his eyes.

"He's alive, he's alive!" she shouted. She picked up the boy and carried him to the emergency department.

The boy, who had brain matter coming out of his ears, was immediately taken to the operating room. The boy lived! This is just one of the many miracles that happened that night.

But in the midst of everything, God is good. He is restoring a hopeless city. He is making all things new again and He is here to carry us into the light.

My house, although it had been destroyed, was rebuilt. My insurance paid for the house and all the valuables within it. I started receiving checks from unknown charities. Everything was coming back into focus. God was truly taking care of me.

I started viewing God differently at that point. I knew, in spite of all the chaos in my life, there was something else out there for me, something I had wanted for a long time. I started searching. Where would I find God? Well, the only place I knew of was church, so I went. I started "church hopping" in hopes of finding what it was I was looking for. Although I knew of God and had started praying to Him, I still didn't know what God was all about. I knew I had to search for Him.

I went to multiple churches with people I knew who were close to God, and I started to feel a tug in my heart. I started to see God's glory and it was beautiful. I knew then that this was the something I had been looking for. I asked God, "Place me somewhere where I can fit in."

As the months went on, I gave my life to Christ. I really did. I decided I would no longer be an addict and to discontinue hanging with the same people who influenced me to turn back into the darkness. Deciding to make it publicly known, I got baptized. I was baptized in September of 2012—eleven years after I had decided to quit meth. It took some time, but I believe it was all in God's timing. From the moment I stepped out of the water, I knew my life was changed forever.

Things started happening. I found where I fit at Destiny Church. I was asked to be in leadership with the young adult ministry, called GAP412. God had showed me where I fit in!

And then God gave me someone to share my life with—Emily. Emily was so beautiful when I first saw her at work. And, of course, she couldn't get past my charm. We became inseparable, so we decided to get married. After marriage, we decided to dedicate our lives to the Lord. We're not perfect, but we keep our focus on God and He manages everything.

Marriage is a beautiful thing. God intended for marriage to be good. Our lives with God are one big marriage. We have God, the groom, and the church, His bride, in complete accord. We keep our eyes on God and He keeps His eyes always on us, His children.

I love what God has done in my life, through all the suffering and through the good times. He is glorious! His purpose for your life is to know Him. Life is a gift, and while you are enjoying your gift, God wants to be there as you open it. He says, "Enjoy what I have brought you." Yes, times are difficult, and we have a lot of questions about life, but God wants us to trust in Him in everything we do. He will take care of the rest. That's exactly what God is— He is love. And there is an infinite supply of Him.

9

Perfect Love

ere I am, a changed man. Let me tell you, it has been one unbelievable ride. I have shared with you stories and chapters in my life which line up into one big journey. Life is a journey. It's a complete rollercoaster sometimes, but it is a gift. You probably have a lot of questions, like why did I go through such torture, why didn't I hide from the darkness, and why did it take so long for me to find God? But isn't time all we have here on earth? There is,

> *A time to be born and a time to die, a time to plant and a time to uproot, a time to kill and a time to heal, a time to tear down and a time to build, a time to weep and a time to laugh, a time to mourn and a time to dance, a time to scatter stones and a time to gather them, a time to embrace and a time to refrain from embracing, a time to search and a time to give up, a time to keep and a time to throw away, a time to tear and a time to mend, a time to be silent and a time to*

speak, a time to love and a time to hate, a time for war and a time for peace, (Ecclesiastes 3:1-8).

As you can see, there is a time for everything. A thousand days in Heaven is like one day on earth. Time is of the essence, but God doesn't measure time. He measures the love He has for you.

If I could sum up this book by taking all the defiance, all the fear, all the heartache, all the suffering, all the conquering, all the glory, all the revelations, and all that God has given me, I would place it together under one title—love. Love is the reason we exist. We exist to be loved and to love others. I know what you're thinking: "But the world is a terrible place." And I would have to agree with you. Let me take you on a journey through our ancestors who have passed along their legacy up to now. In the beginning, God created the heavens and the earth. He said, "Let there be light," and there it was. God saw that everything He created was good, so after six days of creating the earth, the land, the waters, and all creation, He made man. But He didn't just make man, He made man in His image—in God's *complete* image! He created Adam to have all authority and dominion over the earth and its creatures. But He didn't want to leave Adam alone, so He created woman to be with man. He created Eve to fellowship and be in communion with Adam.

God gave everything to Adam and Eve. They were in complete harmony with one another as they loved God and took care of His garden. The world was in complete alignment with God, and it was beautiful. But something happened: a serpent—the devil—came to tempt Eve. He told her if she ate from the tree of knowledge, the one tree God told them *not* to eat from, they would gain all the knowledge and power of God. They rebelled against God and ate the fruit of the tree. They then noticed how naked they were and hid from God. God called out, "Where are you?" The couple still hid.

God wasn't there to punish them. He wanted them to come back to Him so they could continue their journey together, but they felt so ashamed and guilty for disobeying God.

Generations came and went and sin continued to increase within the earth. The first murder happened among the children of Adam and Eve, and sin spread like a wildfire. The earth was so dark that God told Noah He was going to bring a flood and start over. Noah obeyed God and built an ark. After the floods came and the earth was washed clean, Noah and his family had to start over.

God said, "I will establish my covenant with you, never again will all life be destroyed by the waters of a flood; never again will there be a flood to destroy the earth," (Genesis 9:11). "I have set my rainbow in the clouds, and it will be the sign of the covenant between me and the earth," (Genesis 9:13). Isn't that amazing? God said He would never flood the earth again and would show you His promise by revealing a rainbow.

As you would imagine, life was once again restored, but sin and darkness came again. Yet, God holds onto His promises because He is righteous. God knew we couldn't protect ourselves from sin, so He sent a Savior, Jesus Christ. Some nonbelievers and skeptics believe Jesus was a great prophet and teacher, but you have to understand He came to save us. Jesus's specific purpose on this earth was to save us from our own selves. He was the Son of God in human flesh, who taught the Word of God, performed miracles, forgave all sinners, and showed the love of the Father. He was the demonstration of God's love. "While we were still sinners, Christ died for us," (Romans 5:8). Isn't that amazing? Even though we are filled with darkness because of our ancestor's rebellion, God still adores us. God still adored those young boys who beat me back at church camp. Although they were trying to build confidence through their fists, God still forgives, and I forgave them as well.

After Christ was crucified on the cross, everything changed. Everything! Before Christ died, He cried out, "It is finished!" (John 19:30). That meant your sins and mine are forgiven and there is a new promise, a new priesthood, a new way, and a new life to live. We no longer have to live in darkness, because He has moved us out into the light. We no longer have to sulk in our own sorrows, because we have a Savior to pick us back up. Our pain is His strength, and there is no better time to give your life to Him than right now.

So where are you right now with God? At this very moment, what is your relationship with Him? I don't care about your background and those who have hurt you in the church. I don't care about what cards you have been dealt in life that you can't discard. I don't care how dark your life is right now because God will pick you back up so you can start again. He wants to restart a new life with you that is filled with an abundance of His goodness. He wants to start right where you left off with Him, and if you have never believed in Jesus before, I would love to invite you into a relationship that is so vast, so deep, so wide, so apparent, and so wonderful that you will never ever turn back to your old life again. That old life will mean nothing when you experience the blood of Jesus.

I have seen darkness, I have seen hell, and I have walked with demons, but through all the chaos and tribulations in my life, God has always been there for me. Always. It just took some time for me to turn back to Him and surrender my life fully. I know what you're thinking, "But I'm afraid of change." That's okay. Surrendering is never an easy thing, not at first.

However, the more you build your relationship with God, the more you want to surrender.

This book is called *Coincidence or God?* In it, I have revealed to you my life-changing transformation story, but I want you to understand how much God is in complete control of your life and this life is not a coincidence. I'm going to tell you a few more personal stories that emphasize there are no coincidences in life. These stories are one-hundred percent true, so read them and really digest them.

Meet Noah. Noah is a little rough around the edges. Noah looks like he could bench press a Mack truck. Seriously, this guy is large. One night, while I was finishing up a twelve-hour shift, I got the urge to go the gym and work out. After twelve hours in the emergency room? Yeah, I had a lot of motivation that day. I entered through the doors of the gym, and there was Noah, curling a sixty-pound dumbbell. I walked right up to him and started curling along with him.

"Hey, man, how are you doing?" I asked.

"Not so good," he replied.

"What's going on?"

Noah began to open up to me about his baby's momma who had left him and taken his child. He told me he had been contemplating suicide.

My heart sank. I saw his heart being crushed by the situation surrounding him. I got his number and told him I was there for him and wanted to help in any way I could. We talked and texted all night long and I could feel the pain this man was enduring.

The next morning, I woke to a text from Noah. I decided to drive over to his house to pick him up so we could talk. We drove around talking about life. I told him my life had been completely changed since I gave my life to God, that I had been a meth addict for six years, and I had lived a very dark life. He'd heard a little about God, but wanted to know more, so I continued talking about the goodness that comes from Him. Noah then opened up and admitted he was abusive toward his baby's momma and he wanted to change his life. After hours of talking with Noah, I dropped him off back at his house.

I went back home and started reading The Bible. Then something happened. I heard a knock at my door. I opened the door and there was Noah.

He asked if could come in.

"Sure, sure come in, Noah," I said.

He sat down, almost in tears, and talked about how messed up his life was, how much pain he had caused others, and how he wanted to change. He then said some of the strongest words I had ever heard, "Aaron, can you help me get right with God and get saved?"

I could not believe what I had just heard. "Yes, yes I would *love* to help you!" I said.

Noah gave his life to God that day, right in the middle of my living room. He shouted out, "God, come into my life. I need you." The weight on Noah's shoulders began to lessen. He was being set free! When someone gives his or her life to Christ there is a celebration in Heaven among the angels, and Noah and I rejoiced together that day as we welcomed him into the family of God.

If you think that was a coincidence, let's go a little deeper. Meet Peter. Peter, who is a man on fire for God, was working out at the gym (a different gym). I was working out and had set my Monster Energy® drink aside.

Peter was walking by and kicked my drink over accidentally. "I'm sorry, man, I'm sorry," he said.

"Not a big deal, man," I replied.

This accident caused us to strike up a conversation about God and all His glory. We started texting each other and became great friends.

Peter has a passion for the lost. He himself was once in the darkness. He has multiple convictions he spent time in prison for, but he is very open about his history because it makes for a great testimony of what God has done in his life. Peter spends most of his time at the local cigar bar in Joplin. He sits with Atheists and Agnostics, Buddhists and Muslims, and he speaks the goodness of Jesus Christ. I know what you're thinking, "He preaches in the middle of a bar?" That's exactly what he is doing. Jesus never told us to stay in our Christian bubbles. He said, "Go out unto the world and preach the gospel to all creation,"

(Mark 16:15). Jesus Himself sat with sinners because He was the closest thing to the Word of God that anybody had ever seen. We, as in the image of Christ, should sit among sinners and love them because we are the closest thing to a Bible these men and women will ever have.

I stepped on board with Peter. We set up shop right in the middle of all the darkness and spoke the good news to everyone we encountered. But God wanted to go deeper. As Peter was driving by the bar district in Joplin one night, God spoke to him, "Why aren't you reaching those people?" Wow, God was right. Where would Jesus be today if He walked on the earth? He would be right in the middle of the darkest places, among the lost and the unsaved. He would go where the Word of God needs to infiltrate.

Peter and I went there, and supernatural things started happening. We spoke with an entire generation of Atheists and Agnostics—a sea of men and women who didn't believe in a God who does exist. They all have terrible stories and I feel each one's pain, but I can't allow the enemy to take their lives, so Peter and I speak life into them. We are not there to convict them or try to convert them, but to share the love of Christ through our lives. Men and women are now rededicating their lives to the Lord. But with the light, comes darkness. We recently encountered evil spirits there. A dark-eyed woman approached us, rambling about how she was going to "annihilate us" and "melt us." She was speaking evil words, but we didn't back down because we had the Holy Spirit with us and that Spirit is far greater than anything of this world. "Greater is He that is in you, than he that is in the world," (1 John 4:4).

We call ourselves "Nightwalkers." It's a great ministry and it's growing. Christians are stepping out in faith and joining the great commission by spreading the gospel to the lost, oppressed, and unsaved. I'm beyond thankful to God for aligning me with the right people at just the right time to increase the Kingdom of Heaven.

God has also connected me with other believers who want to reach more of the community. We feed the homeless, clothe the poor, and minister to many individuals. While we were handing out hot cocoa to the poor one day, God talked to us through prayer about salvations. That day, seventeen homeless people rededicated their lives to Christ, and two men, who were Atheists, gave their lives to God for the first time. We don't want to just enable the homeless; we want to set them free. All around the community we have started doing "treasure hunts" with a group of believers who receive instructions from God, with descriptions, and we go out to the mall, Walmart, or wherever God tells us that day and we pray for people and let them know that *they* are God's treasure. We've gotten some amazing results.

I could go on and on regarding the testimonies God has given me, but this book cannot contain the glory of God, who desperately wants to know all His children. I'm not trying to boast about all the things God has done through me, but I want to show you the supernatural deliveries God is doing in my life. He has set a fire within my heart and I can't contain the goodness He is bringing about. That is the same fire He wants to ignite within your heart. All it takes is surrendering your life to Him and saying out loud, "God, I'm ready to do your will." Isaiah 6:8 paints a picture of when Isaiah heard the voice of the Lord ask, "Whom shall I send?" And Isaiah shouted out, "Send me God."

God is looking for thirsty and hungry men and women who are willing to *give up* their lives to *have* life. It begins with a relationship—an intimate oneness. He is looking for people who wake up every day knowing that no matter what happens in the day, they will trust in the Lord.

Here we are at the conclusion of my book, and you probably still have a lot of questions. Why do I go through so much pain? Why doesn't my family accept me? Why doesn't anything ever go my way? Remember this, "And we know that in all things God works for the good of those who love Him, who have been called according to His purpose," (Romans 8:28). No matter what you have been through in life, and are still going through, God is always with you.

This means you have protection, you have confidence, and you have power and authority over every situation and obstacle if you are in relationship with God. What was intended to be bad, God uses for the good of those who love Him. God has used me.

I know this is true because God has started using me to mentor to other addicts who are going through the same things I went through. I started an addiction recovery support group for people to come together in oneness and hold each other accountable.

There is so much darkness out there and it is important we stay deep in the Word of God to protect us from evil. I still, to this day, fight my temptations, but I have God to get me through the difficulties. I completely rely on His grace. I'm not saying it's an easy walk. It was easier to *find* Jesus than it is to *follow* Jesus, but the greatest part is that God will never leave you or forsake you. It's His promise, and God can't go against His own word.

I want to invite you into a new life with new meaning. I'm not saying it will be easy, but I do promise you it will be worth everything. You just have to acknowledge there is a God who deeply loves you and wants to know you more. It's never too late. Whether you're sitting in your living room, at the desk in your office, driving in your car, sitting on the street, or you're in the middle of nowhere, you can have Him right now—right at this very moment. God's love can't be contained, it's infinite. It's welcoming, and He has His arms stretched wide. He awaits your arrival. "Ask and it will be given to you; seek and you will find; knock and the door will be opened to you. For everyone who asks receives; the one who seeks finds; and to the one who knocks, the door will be opened," (Matthew 7:7-8). Crack open the door to His existence and you will see Him. He has prepared a feast to satisfy you. His love is never-ending. It never stops. This is the reason why you were born—to know God and to be loved by Him.

I wouldn't change one thing about my life. After all, it's what made me who I am. All the situations, all the problems, all the goodness, all the chapters, all of my life God used to mold me into His image, and it's been one heck of a ride. The day I gave my life to the Lord was the greatest day of my life. The night I was down in the devil's den, completely surrounded by darkness, was the very place God came to deliver me. He said, "This is my son, who I love very much." Ever since that night, I have been thankful for the revelation He gave me. I fall more and more in love with God every day. He tells me all the time, "Don't forget from where I brought you." I *never* forget from where He has brought me. There's always a Bible verse that can describe where you are in life or that completely describes you. Mine is Psalms 118:5, "I called upon the Lord in distress, the Lord answered, and set me in a higher place." That's exactly what He is doing in my life. Amen.

Acknowledgements

I would like to take this time to acknowledge my parents for always believing in me. You never gave up on who I was, and this book is a product of your love. To Pastor Gene Bebee, thank you for your spiritual guidance and wisdom, the leadership that you have provided has set me up for success. JD Buckridge, you will never understand how much you helped me become the Godly man that I am now. This book is a harvest of the seeds that you planted within me. To all my brothers and sister in Christ, thank you for your encouragement, love, compassion, and perseverance. Let's set a fire down in our hearts for God that we can't contain, that we can't control!

Author Bio

Author Aaron Garcia is an inspirational writer and video blogger. He is an addiction life specialist and support group leader of the ministry "Restored" through Destiny Church. Aaron mentors to men who suffer from addiction and gives back to the community by feeding and ministering to the homeless. Aaron has been a Registered Nurse for seven years, has his Bachelor of Science in Nursing, and is currently pursuing his Masters in Nursing. Aaron and his wife, Emily, reside in Joplin, Missouri where he has lived most of his life.

Made in the USA
Lexington, KY
28 October 2019